THE THINKING PROBLEM

101 Journal Prompts to Discover the
Secret Behind Self-Efficacy and Your Success

PARIS RYAN

Kendall Hunt
publishing company

Dedication

This book is dedicated to my beautiful canine children, Rowdy, Missy, Kaley, and Brody, and for my children who I am yet to meet but have always loved. Thank you for being my greatest accomplishments and for changing my own self-efficacy in every way it could have been changed. As I always say, being your mother is the greatest title, job, and adventure I have ever had. I love you, always and forever, and more than the sun, and the moon, and the stars combined. Everything I am is because of you, because I love you, and because I am loved by you.

CONTENTS

ABOUT THE AUTHOR

Dr. Paris Ryan has a bachelor's and master's degree in English literature with an emphasis in creative writing, and a doctorate in educational leadership with a focus on higher education. While earning her master's degree, she was an editor for a local lifestyle magazine called *Style* and was the photojournalist and columnist for The Sacramento Bee's cocktail column called *Nightlife*, which focused on the best happy hours in the area.

© Latha Narayan

Her doctoral dissertation, *Is Writing a Self-Perception Problem? Self-Efficacy and Student Success in First-Year Composition*, focused on self-efficacy and student success in college composition, while her first book, *Composing Composition: The Art of the Written Word*, focused on how to improve your scholarly writing and how to write various types of academic essays.

She currently works as an English professor in sunny San Diego, CA and sits on the National Advisory Council for the National Conference on Race and Ethnicity in American Higher Education. While she has taught students from P-12 to doctoral candidates, she likes spending most of her time teaching students who are attending community college. As the "Doctor of Self-Efficacy," her goal is to help you improve your own mindset and make your wildest dreams into reality. When she is not in the classroom, you can find her writing, presenting research at regional and national conferences, traveling the world, or hanging out by the beach with her Chihuahua (and co-author), Brody.

ACKNOWLEDGMENTS

When I was 15, I could not run a mile and thought that running a marathon would be an incredible thing to say, but an impossible thing to accomplish. When I was 19, I dreamt that I would become a doctor but doubted my own abilities because I was not sure I had the ability to get into graduate school. And when I was 25, I thought that the only way I could ever write a book before I turned 30 was if I self-published it. But the thing each of these has in common is that my self-efficacy about my own abilities was wrong. I ran a marathon, became a doctor, and wrote a book called *Composing Composition: The Art of the Written Word*. However, they also had another thing in common and that was the fact that I did not achieve any of these accomplishments by myself. During my doctoral program interviews, in my dissertation, and in my first book, I shared the African proverb that I have always loved and lived by: "It takes a village to raise a child." And that is because it does take a village to do so many things, from graduating from school to writing a book or accomplishing any of our wildest dreams. Thus, I am very grateful to my village who helped me make this dream come true and supported me making this labor of love into a reality.

To my students, former, current, and future, thank you for allowing me to be your professor. Watching you grow as writers and work on improving your self-efficacy is my greatest privilege, and I hope *The Thinking Problem: 101 Journal Prompts to Discover the Secret Behind Self-Efficacy and Your Success*, will help transform your mindset when it comes to writing or whatever else you dream of every day.

To my publisher and editorial team at Kendall Hunt, thank you for not just finding me, but for guiding me through this process, and being so patient as I worked on this book. Thank you especially to Emi Sneed and Rachel Guhin, as well as my former Author Account Managers and Editors: Lara Sanders, Megan Drake, and Caitlin Simas for all of our editorial meetings, responding to the plethora of questions I always have, and allowing me to be a part of the publishing process with you. It was an incredible experience and I loved every moment of it.

To my family, thank you for helping me accomplish my greatest dreams, from writing two books to becoming a doctor. To my mother, Latha Narayan, my father, Ananth Narain, and my brother, Krishna Narayan, thank you for being my original village.

And most of all, thank you to my beautiful children. You are my greatest inspirations and the reason I wrote this book. You are all in my heart every day, even if once again, I only had Brody in my arms. Rowdy's Rule, Missy's Memoir, Kaley's Quiz, and Brody's Breakdown are my dedication to you. And to my sweet R and M, as I said in Le Diss, aka my doctoral dissertation, my R-Model and Motivation Theory were only ever inspired and created because of the two of you.

And lastly, as I wrote in my dissertation, to anyone who ever has suffered from low self-efficacy in something – whether it is writing, starting a business, winning an Oscar, or something else entirely – you are the ones who inspired me to fall in love with the topic of self-efficacy. I hope this book helps you strengthen your self-efficacy and reframes your belief system so that you recognize that you can accomplish anything your heart desires. As I wrote in Le Diss, "…Henry Ford once said, 'whether you think you can, or you think you can't – you're right.' And I know you can, and will, be more successful than your wildest of dreams." And as I always say, it is time for us to stop dreaming and start doing. So here's to you and our wildest, most beautiful dreams becoming our reality.

PART I

Introduction

{The key to success comes from within}

When I began my doctoral program, I knew I would eventually write a dissertation. My fear of *le diss*, as I lovingly named my dissertation, was never about writing a book of research that spanned between 100 and 400 pages; my fear was writing about relevant, interesting, and important research that felt engaging and easy to comprehend. I did not want a dissertation written just for the sake of the title that would make me a doctor; I wanted a dissertation that mattered, that would influence my pedagogical and andragogical practices, and one that could become a book (like this one) eventually. The idea of writing about research that interested me and that was important for society was my main goal, which is why I wrote it on self-efficacy and its impact on our success.

At the start of the semester I teach all my students about self-efficacy. And it is something we continue to discuss as the semester progresses anytime a student says something such as, *"I suck at grammar"* or *"I cannot write well."* Self-efficacy, at its core, is about finding our true, authentic confidence. It is about creating a belief system where we believe that we can and will be successful at a given task. And this book is about building that belief system.

Self-efficacy impacts our success in everything we do. Whether I believe I can start a multimillion-dollar company, teach undergraduate students, write this book, or have successful social relationships, everything we do stems from our self-confidence and belief that we are capable of succeeding. The research in this book will prove that and expand into why that matters and how we can create a change for ourselves and for others. Self-efficacy may not be a new subject, but this book combines research and theory and expands into why self-efficacy matters.

When I was a child, I had a four-question method for whether or not I should buy something. I taught it to my mom and whenever we would go shopping and she questioned whether she should buy the item and allow it to take up space in her beautifully curated home, I would recite my questions back to her. My questions were: *Do you love it? Do you need it? Do you want it? And is the price right?*

I always asked the questions in this order since if I did not love something, what was the point of buying it, even if I needed it? After all, I could always find the item I needed, such as dinner plates, that I also loved due to their beautiful pattern. If I did not want the item, why was I considering buying it and bringing it into my home? And of course, if the price was not right, I likely would not invest my money on something no matter how much I loved it. After all, even if I found a dress I loved, needed for an event, and wanted, I was unlikely to pay a price that was beyond my budget. My mother loved this approach and always answered my questions as we admired the various items in a store. Whether it was investing in a dainty gold necklace at the gold souk in Dubai, or buying a simple couch for my living room in California, I have found that these questions have lasted the test of time.

Marie Kondo created an empire out of a similar philosophy when it comes to keeping your home curated. Unlike my idea of not buying an item unless it was necessary – a principle that likely led to my love of all things minimalist – Kondo's practice led to the idea of whether the items we already own and weigh us down lead to them *sparking joy*. Kondo's principle is simple, effective, and a lovely way of viewing our closets, pantries, and homes, and a reason why she has created a multimillion dollar empire, multiple books, a TV show, and a movement out of items that bring us joy being the things we need in our home. But you are likely wondering why I am discussing shopping and curating our physical possessions in a book you picked up to better understand your self-efficacy and discover your authentic confidence when it comes to your writing abilities and beyond.

My dear friend, a fellow writer and former English professor, Erica Spriggs, told me a brilliant tip she teaches her students every semester. She advises them to "Marie Kondo their papers." Her meaning behind that is to have them remove aspects of their essay that does not spark joy or seems to create unnecessary clutter such as a paragraph long hook that can be shortened to just one or two sentences. This fits in with removing aspects of an essay that you do not love.

After all, students often can tell what they earned on a paper before their professor grades it, and there is no better feeling than working hard on something and having that work be recognized. But after pondering on Erica's pedagogical (and in our case with college students, andragogical) practice, I recognized that we could use this philosophy when it comes to self-efficacy and authentic confidence as well. And while we can, as she says, "Marie Kondo" these aspects of our life, we will also delve into questions we can ask ourselves to build on our self-efficacy and our success. After all, as a child I utilized a series of questions when it came to shopping (and I honestly still do the same today), so I believe in creating a series of questions to boost our authentic confidence as well.

While our self-confidence and self-efficacy are aspects of ourselves that we need to work on every day of our lives, this book will delve into ways we can declutter our negative thoughts, remove beliefs that do not spark joy from our psyche, and find the questions we must ask to decide whether or not our mindset is worth keeping. While writing and shopping can seem like two different things, only related in the sense that some of us, like myself, enjoy the two, I always go back to the questions my 11-year-old self asked my mother when we went shopping, even when I work on my inner confidence today. After all, if I do not *love* the way I view myself, I know to get rid of it from my mind. It is simply creating unnecessary clutter. If I do not *need* the way I think of myself, such as with a negative view, then I need to get rid of it. And while our thoughts may not have a monetary cost, they do come at a price. And if the *price is not right*, then I need to get rid of it instead of wasting my energy on something that will never benefit me.

This book will delve into how low self-efficacy and self-confidence, and high self-apprehensiveness will never behoove anyone. Starting today we will change our thoughts from *I cannot, I suck at, I fail,* and other self-doubting beliefs, to *I am working on improving my ability (to do said task)*. Part 1 of The *Thinking Problem* teaches you the research behind confidence, self-efficacy, imposter syndrome, fear, and understanding how we affect other people's self-efficacy and how they can impact our own, while Part 2 allows you to journal your way to a stronger self-efficacy. And while this book focuses on writing, namely in academia, I want you to recognize that these thoughts go well beyond just our writing capabilities and into every aspect of our lives. So let us clean up the clutter in our minds and fill it with only positive, self-affirming thoughts to help us succeed. After all, as Henry Ford once said, "Whether you think you can or you think you can't, you're right." And Ford was definitely correct about this.

{It all comes down to how we view ourselves. So, do you see yourself as the cat or the lion?}

© canbedone/Shutterstock.com

Rowdy's Rule: *Both confidence and self-efficacy are based on your behavior. They are not a personality trait or something we are either born with or without. Thus, everyone can improve their confidence and increase their self-efficacy if they choose to work on it every day.*

Audrey Hepburn's famous quote, "Nothing is impossible, the word itself says 'I'm possible'" always reminds me of the power of confidence and of a child's belief in themselves. After all, if you were to ask a child, they would likely tell you that nothing is impossible. Whether you want to be a movie star, an astronaut, or a professional athlete, children never doubt their abilities on how to make their wildest dreams into a reality. It is part of what makes childhood seem so magical, because after that time period where our imaginations can dictate our realities, we begin to doubt our ability to succeed at even the simplest of things.

Confidence can often feel like something that can be so elusive. We all know someone who seems to have it, yet most of us struggle with it in some aspect of our life. In fact, according to the *New York Post* in 2020, a survey of 2,000 Americans found that 59% are insecure when it comes to their appearance, with body image, skin issues, poorly fitting clothes, and social media being the culprits that caused their lack of confidence (Sandlier 2020). Another article from *NBC News* in 2017 stated that 85% of people suffer from low self-esteem (Alton 2017). This can result in them earning less money, avoiding entrepreneurial pursuits, and taking fewer financial risks over the course of their lives. Even in Canada, a 2019 article from *Ipsos* shares a survey that showed that 40% of teenagers lack confidence when it comes to social situations, which causes them to avoid trying to meet new people ("Four in Ten Canadians (40%) Lack Confidence in Social Situations" 2019). Yet, on the flip side, there are magazine articles, websites, and books for all ages focusing on boosting one's confidence. We can all likely come to one common conclusion: confidence is important for our success and happiness, while overconfidence and underconfidence will negatively impact our lives.

They say confidence is the most attractive quality a person can have, but how do you define it? Is it something you are born with or something you work on every day? Is it something you believe you have or is it something you struggle with? And what is the most recent thing in your life that made you feel confident? Take a minute to think about this. Did you come up with a situation quickly or did it take you a bit of time to come up with something? And how recent was your event? Did it happen today, yesterday, two months ago, or two minutes ago?

I have always found confidence to be a fascinating aspect of psychology. But when I began my doctoral program, I realized that I was the only one out of my entire cohort who did not dread writing my qualifying exam (which was not going to happen for another two years) and who was excited to write my dissertation. I was also the only person in that room that late August evening who felt my writing was at the doctoral level, even though I was the youngest in my program. While I had spent a few years working as a journalist before beginning this program, I was not the only English major in that room. My peers were other educators, including English professors and community college vice presidents. This was when I became even more fascinated by the idea of self-efficacy, which Albert Bandura defined as a person's belief in his or her ability to succeed at a given task. I realized in that moment that we all struggle with aspects of self-efficacy; for me, it had always been math, and for my classmates, it was writing.

Self-efficacy goes beyond just academics as well. Low self-efficacy can be what stops us from chasing our dreams of becoming the movie star or astronaut we wanted to be as children, scares us into sticking with the status quo instead of starting the company we always wanted to run and becoming our own boss, or even gets us to doubt our ability to do things like move somewhere new or become a great cook. And yet, when we have high self-efficacy, we can find ourselves pursuing the things we once swore were impossible. And we will find ourselves succeeding at the impossible. The best part of it to me though, is that self-efficacy, like confidence, is a behavior and not a personality trait. This means that with a set intention and practice, everyone can transform their self-efficacy over time and make the impossible, possible.

So how do we change our confidence and our self-efficacy? It is not easy and it is something we must work on daily to improve. But it is worth it.

10 Ways to Increase Your Self-Confidence

1. **Focus on the smaller wins to win the bigger wins.** The root of low self-efficacy goes back to failure. Focus on smaller tasks first, ones where you are more likely to succeed. For example, the Motivation Theory, as I theorized in my dissertation, formulated that low-risk assignments, such as short readings and writing assignments such as free writing and journaling, alongside other aspects that the teacher focuses on, would positively impact and improve the self-efficacy of a student. Thus, focus first on smaller tasks such as journaling before trying to tackle the essay. If you start succeeding at the "lower risk assignments," the ones that are not worth as many points (and thus are less stressful), your self-efficacy will increase as you move toward the higher risk assignments like your essays and final exams.

2. **Take note of your successes.** It can help to have a list of your successes that you look at any time your self-esteem plummets, or to even write each success down on a piece of paper and

{They say confidence is key. That it is the most attractive quality a person can possess. And that it is necessary for success. So how do you find your confidence from within?}

put all those papers in a jar. Anytime you feel your confidence level dips, you can pick out one, two, three, or however many successes from the jar to remember just how much you have done.

3. **Reframe failure.** I love making mistakes because I never forget a lesson — I learn from it. When I was in middle school, my favorite way to study for spelling tests was to quiz my friends before class. Whenever any of us made a mistake, I would forever remember how to spell that word. This trick even got me all the way to our regional spelling bee. I still find it works today. If I baked cookies and accidentally added too much butter or not enough sugar, I would never forget that mistake. If I miss a meeting I meant to attend, I would never again forget to mark it down in my planner and get there early. However, with low self-efficacy, it can be easy to consider the failure as a personal failure. But getting an F on an essay or exam, not getting a loan for your business plan, or moving to a new state only to find you hate it there, is not a personal failure. It is life. If it never rained, we would never have rainbows, and if we never failed a paper, we could never appreciate the joy of getting that A. Failure is simply a learning experience and a part of life. It is not something to fear. And it is definitely not something that you should allow to impact your success and happiness.

4. **Fake it until you make it.** No one is born confident. It is a skill we develop as we grow up. If you think about it, even the fittest person likely has some sort of insecurity when it comes to their body. Even the most beautiful person likely has days where they just cannot stand their skin or hair or appearance. And even the smartest, most successful person likely feels silly, or like an imposter at some point in their career. But it is our job to pretend that we are the most confident, fit, beautiful, intelligent, and successful person every day, even on, or really especially on, the days we most doubt ourselves. You might be surprised to find yourself not having to fake it after awhile because it will become your new normal way of thinking.

5. **Believe in yourself.** The truth is you are amazing and the only reason you have to doubt your ability at something is because it is an option for you to either pursue or run away from. If you are in a college composition classroom, that means you are ready to succeed in that class according to your college, your professor, and your peers. You would not be in the class if you were not ready for it. After all, were you able to take a college level class in third grade?

6. **Remember that everyone makes mistakes.** It can be so easy to get disappointed when we make a mistake. Whether it is a spelling error in our well-written paper or it is forgetting that we have our final essay due on Tuesday, it is important to remember that we all make errors. The important part of these failures is to make sure we learn from them instead of allowing such obstacles to destroy our self-worth, self-esteem, and confidence. Failing a class, for example, can easily make us feel truly awful about our capability in that class and subject. However, a grade does not define us, and if we are able to learn why we failed (due to missing class, skipping assignments, or not reaching out and seeking help on the course), it could be a good thing that happened to us.

7. **Focus on what you can do.** While you may come into an English class with low self-efficacy and low confidence levels due to how you feel about your own writing, how you feel about

English as a subject, or something else entirely, it is essential to consider the things you can do. While your confidence when it comes to writing might not change overnight, you can choose to focus on having a tutor review your paper or reaching out to your professor for additional help. By focusing on the things you can do, you can slowly improve your writing over the course of the semester, and thus increase your confidence levels when you see yourself succeed.

8. **Ignore your inner Negative Nancy or Negative Neil.** We all have an internal voice that sometimes is not our greatest cheerleader. Maybe you call this voice Negative Nancy or Neil, or Debbie or Dan Downer, but even if it feels like no one else has a voice like this, the truth is, we all do. It is our job to stop listening to the negative soundtrack in our mind. Perhaps you distract yourself with a long run, a call with your best friend, or having a dance party with your dog. Whatever works for you, find a way to quiet down the pessimistic voices that try to destroy your confidence and self-esteem.

9. **Create your own cheerleader.** We may all deal with our Nancy or Neil, but they do not have to be the only voice we hear. Remember how in cartoons they would show an angel and a devil on the protagonist's shoulders? The angel wanted to convince our hero or heroine to do the right thing, while the devil wanted them to do the fun, naughty thing. It is our job to create our own cheerleader for whenever we hear our negative voice. So, to counteract your Negative Nancy or Dan Downer, aside from finding a way to distract yourself from their voice, create your own cheerleader such as Paul or Paula Positive, or Optimistic Oliver or Olivia.

10. **Remember the confidence you do have.** To simply live, we all have to have some amount of confidence. Whether it is making a decision on what to eat, what to wear, or what you want to do that day, our daily decisions (which we make hundreds of every day) require a certain amount of confidence. For instance, a salad that is healthy, nutritious, and made with your homemade bleu cheese dressing, or a pizza that is delicious, made entirely from scratch, and handcrafted with fresh tomatoes and basil from your backyard garden, can make you feel instantly confident since you know you are making something for yourself that only you can do (does everyone have your bleu cheese dressing recipe or a backyard garden?). Another example could be choosing to wear your favorite pair of jeans this morning since you instantly know that they are comfortable, fit well, and make you feel great. Each of these decisions we make can be a gentle reminder of the confidence we already possess.

Missy's Memoir

{How do other people impact your confidence?}

Missy is a college student who lives with her best friend and roommate, Kaley, and has many adventures with Kaley and their friends, Rowdy and Brody. Throughout this book, we will see some of her adventures as she navigates the waters of being a student and increasing her own self-efficacy.

"Have you finished the paper for English yet?" Kaley inquires. Kaley and Missy are sitting in their living room for their Sunday study day with Brody and Rowdy.

"I finished it last week," Brody states proudly. "I would love to say it was because I am an over-achiever, but really I just did not want to study for math," he chuckles.

"That is called being an overachiever," Missy responds. "I would have gone shopping if I wanted to avoid studying for math." Everyone chuckles knowing that 1) shopping is Missy's cardio, therapy, and favorite hobby, and 2) she is correct. Brody is an overachiever and he likely has written the best paper in their class.

"I began it," Rowdy shares. "I just feel really stuck, like a bad case of writer's block, so I am free writing right now to try and get some new ideas. How about you, Kay? Miss?" Missy tries to hide her face in her book, pretending to be reading it intently instead of paying attention. Kaley sees this and immediately responds.

"I have my outline completed and I was going to try and get my first draft done today. Since it is due at the end of the week, I figure I can get a couple of drafts done, share the paper with

Professor Collins during office hours at the start of the week, and put the finishing touches by Thursday evening so I can get my full eight hours of sleep before class on Friday. At least, that is my hope," Kaley chuckles.

Missy's friends know she does not like their composition class. If it were not a general education requirement, she would never have signed up for it. But they also know that her dislike for the class is why she is always pulling an all-nighter the night before the essay is due.

"And you, Miss?" Rowdy asks, after waiting for a couple of minutes to see if she would say something.

"I am happy to help you with it," Brody responds, looking at his math textbook.

"I will get to it," Missy states. "I just have work due sooner that I need to finish first."

"You just had your biology test on Friday," Kaley responds. "Why are you studying bio when you do not have homework due or a test this week? You do have an essay due though."

"I just," Missy begins. She pauses trying to find the words. "I do not like composition so I want to work on something else. Ideally, we would be at the mall or the movies or even that new sushi restaurant, but since it is our weekly Sunday study day, I figure I should prepare for a class I actually like by reading ahead."

Even though Rowdy is just a few months older than his friends, they all tell him that his big brown eyes show his wisdom and old soul. "Miss," he begins. "You and Brody are more alike than the two of you realize. He chose to avoid studying for his math test last week by finishing this paper and how did you do on it again, B?"

Brody realizes where Rowds is going with this. "I got a C on the math test," he admits. "If I do not get an A on all the other tests and the final in that class, I will not have a 4.0 GPA this semester."

"Exactly," Rowdy shares. "Brody's fear of math has now impacted his grade in that class. You want to study for bio because of your own fear when it comes to writing. But if the two of you worked on your confidence – journaling your feelings, thinking about why the subject makes you so uncomfortable, and practicing and confronting your fear by actually doing the home-work and improving your skills in that subject – then you could increase your self-efficacy and become even more successful in our class."

Brody and Missy look at each other and realize that Rowdy is right.

"Brody," Missy begins. "Can you please help me with this essay? And anytime you want help with our math class, I am happy to assist. We can study together for all the exams so your GPA stays at a 4.0 this semester."

Brody smiles and replies, "That would be amazing, Miss." Then he looks at Rowdy, nods, and says, "Thanks, R." Turning back to Missy he adds, "Now, let us begin working on that essay."

"And," Kaley adds. "Since you are writing this paper so early, I think it calls for a celebration. We should go to that sushi place you mentioned after we finish studying."

"Yes," everyone cheers together before getting back to their studies.

Workbook Questions

1. What ways can one work on increasing their self-efficacy? Why do you think these would help? Explain.

2. What other ways do you think would help increase your self-efficacy (share at least three more methods)? Why do you recommend these methods? Explain.

Kaley's Quiz

1. If you truly do not feel confident, should you fake having confidence (even to yourself)?
   (True)
   False

2. Confidence and self-efficacy are personality traits that a person is born with.
   True
   (False)

3. Self-efficacy and confidence are the same thing.
   True
   (False)

4. A 2020 survey of 2,000 Americans found that 58% were insecure about their appearance. And in a 2017 article, it was stated that 84% of people suffered from low self-esteem and caused them to earn less money that take fewer financial risks over the course of their lifetime.
   True
   (False)

5. Focusing on small wins can help us gain the confidence necessary for the big wins.
   True
   False

Brody's Breakdown

- Overconfidence and underconfidence can negatively impact our success and happiness. We want to work on our confidence.
- Almost everyone, if not everyone, suffers from low self-efficacy in something – whether it is an academic subject, a career objective, or in their personal life.
- If we choose to do so, we can improve our self-efficacy and increase our self-confidence, but it is something that will take practice, work, and effort every day.

{By reframing your thoughts, you can change your self-efficacy, self-confidence, and increase your success. So now do you think you can, or do you think you cannot?}

Rowdy's Rule: *Self-efficacy focuses on YOUR beliefs in YOUR ability to succeed at any given task. Thus, YOU are the only person who can change this belief and mindset YOU have. Anyone else's opinion, thoughts, or words can only influence your belief, but they cannot change it; only you can.*

Henry Ford once said, "Whether you think you can or you think you can't, you're right," and whether or not it was his intention, this quote goes straight to the heart of what self-efficacy is. Self-efficacy is our belief in how well we can perform at a given task. And while we can have high self-efficacy with certain subjects and assignments, we can also struggle with low self-efficacy with other subjects at the same time. I call confidence and self-esteem self-efficacy's siblings because while they are similar, they are also quite different. Self-confidence focuses more on your all-around feeling of yourself and your capabilities, while self-esteem focuses more on how you inherently feel about yourself. And while higher self-efficacy can boost your self-confidence and self-esteem, it is still not quite the same. Self-efficacy does not determine just our ability to write, but everything we do. Whether it is starting a business, earning a degree, becoming a homeowner, or climbing the corporate ladder, our self-efficacy determines how successful we will be at that given task. In this book, we focus on self-efficacy when it comes to our writing skills; however, you can always reword some of the journaling questions to focus on another aspect of your life as well.

If you are wondering how one can have both low and high self-efficacy (after all we do not talk about anyone having both low and high self-esteem), think about this example: a successful businesswoman who has struggled with her weight her whole life. While she may likely feel confident when it comes to making any decisions regarding business – after all she has succeeded at this before – she could feel very unsure about her ability to successfully lose weight since she has struggled with it her whole life. As you can see in this example, the businesswoman has high self-efficacy in one area of her life and low self-efficacy in another. We all are like her. Self-efficacy rules every area of our lives – from earning a degree, learning a language, launching a business, having a successful relationship, and so on. And because it rules every area of our lives, it is easy to see why we are all likely to suffer from low self-efficacy in certain areas of our lives.

There are several ways in which we can go about reframing our self-efficacy. The main way I go about this is by rephrasing my words. Instead of saying, "I suck at this," or "I cannot do that," I reword it to "I am working on improving my ability to do this and that." It is a simple change, yet it is one that forces you to think about what you want to say. It is so easy to state that we cannot do something or that we are terrible at it. Likely we have determined that we are unable to do something due to past failures, leading to a belief that this is something we simply cannot do or cannot do well. It could also have been caused because of someone else's thoughts, actions, or words. While self-efficacy focuses on just our own self, it can be impacted just as easily by someone else, as it can by ourselves. And it can impact everyone around us, not just ourselves. Imagine if Steve Jobs had not created Apple or Jeff Bezos had not created Amazon. Imagine if William Shakespeare had never written a play or Audrey Hepburn had never auditioned for her iconic role as Holly Golightly in *Breakfast at Tiffany's*. If one of these people had chosen to not share their gifts with the world, our world would have looked completely different.

Bandura stated that there are four sources for our self-efficacy: mastery experiences, vicarious experiences, verbal persuasion, and physiological and emotional states (Bandura 1997). Mastery is defined as succeeding in small tasks that lead us to success and mastery at a subject. For example, getting an A on a homework assignment can help boost our self-efficacy when it comes to writing our paper for class. Vicarious experiences focus on our observation of our peers succeeding at the same task. For instance, if your friend gets an A on an exam, you are more likely to feel you can earn an A. Persuasion focuses on our social network and the influence our loved ones, friends, family, teachers, and supervisors can have on our self-efficacy. If you are surrounded by a social environment who believe in your ability to succeed at various tasks and tell you that consistently, you will be more likely to continue to put in the necessary effort to succeed at it. And lastly, our emotions can also determine our self-efficacy. Depression or stress could lower our confidence levels, while more positive emotions may increase our self-efficacy. If we are having a tough day, for example, we may not feel as capable of completing our essay successfully, while if we are having a great day, we could feel as if nothing is impossible. Remember that self-efficacy influences every aspect of our lives and it is something we must work on every day the way we work on our skin care regimen, exercise routine, or practicing a musical instrument. We do not just wake up one day with high levels of self-efficacy; it is something we need to work on daily.

Writing, or whatever else you believe you cannot do, is a thinking problem. So to change your belief system, you need to change your mindset. It will take time, but my rule has always been to avoid words like *I suck* and *I cannot*. Instead, I tell myself, *I am working on improving that skill or subject*. It takes time; I cannot emphasize this enough. There are plenty of times I accidentally say *I suck at technology* or *I cannot do this*. And every time I do, I have to rephrase my words and remind myself that I do not suck at using technology; I simply need to use it more to better understand it. Slowly but surely, your belief system will change, and one day you will go from fearing the idea of an essay to knowing that you can and will succeed at writing an academic paper. Our belief systems are not built overnight. Rephrase how you talk about yourself and how you think because until you change your accepted truth, you cannot change the belief system you have built over the course of your lifetime. Self-efficacy is our inherent belief in our ability to succeed at a given task. By understanding how our fear and apprehension impacts our success, we can directly influence our success at writing or whatever subject or skill we work towards.

I often tell my students that *writing is a muscle*. After all, the more we work it out, the stronger it gets. In that same way, self-efficacy is also a muscle. It can seem sometimes as if confidence is something we are either born with or lack. We see successful people who seem confident in their knowledge when it comes to their field. And of course, we have all seen, or perhaps even felt, like the insecure person who does not have the answer(s) and just wants to get lost in the crowd. But here is what we never see: the confident person working on building their confidence and self-efficacy.

The student in your class who feels confident and proud of his or her ability to write is likely so confident because of a myriad of reasons starting with the fact that they have had their writing skills praised by their parents, professors, and peers in the past. In fact, a huge part of what made me a writer today was the fact that I was informed over and over again that I could write, and that I could write well. Remember, you can do anything, unless you buy into the belief that you are simply incapable of succeeding in that subject, venture, or experience.

10 Ways to Improve Our Self-Efficacy

1. **Reframe your thoughts, words, and actions.** The simplest concept, but the hardest to put into practice, is that by simply reframing our thoughts and what we say or do, we can slowly but surely change our own opinions and beliefs. Imagine if you dislike bananas but every time you see a banana, talk about a banana, or think of a banana, you say you love it. You tell yourself it is the best fruit in the world. You swear you love the flavor, the texture, and the ability to transform it into so many different treats like healthy "ice cream" and banana bread with oodles of chocolate chips. After a while, you will trick your brain into craving bananas and believing you enjoy the fruit.

2. **Work on baby steps towards your goal.** As Bandura stated with his first source for our self-efficacy, mastery is key and comes from small steps that work toward your goal. Before you write the novel, you will write an essay, a paragraph, a sentence, and a word. You need to start with small steps, gain a mastery over these steps, and eventually you will be able to take the bigger steps, while also having the higher self-efficacy we all want.

3. **Be open to feedback.** I always tell students that the most important feedback we can give is constructive feedback. While no one wants to hear what we can do to strengthen our

{The only person who can transform your self-efficacy is the person who looks back at you in the mirror.}

writing, the truth is that without this key information, we will never become better. Remember that our goal is not to be the best at anything; it is to work toward becoming better than we were yesterday. By being open to constructive criticism, your self-efficacy will automatically increase because you will not view feedback as equating to failure. In fact, receiving feedback means that you have something done, which itself is an accomplishment.

4. **Failure is not a bad thing; it is an experience.** As a recovering perfectionist, I will admit that mistakes can be difficult to deal with. However, it is far more important to find a way to learn from your past failures instead of trying to avoid making any mistakes at all. After all, if you learn from your errors, have you actually failed? Recognize that failure is experience and stop viewing it as another reason why you cannot do something or struggle with something.

5. **Perseverance is the key to success.** At its core, success comes from the repetition of small, daily habits. Whether it is choosing a piece of fruit over a pastry for breakfast, walking during your lunch break instead of staying seated, or writing every day instead of convincing yourself that you are not a writer, these habits over time become your daily actions, thoughts, and words. If one day I eat a donut for breakfast, pizza for lunch, and burgers and fries for dinner, my health is not likely to change from what it was the day before. Perhaps I will not feel as well that day, but I will not gain 10 pounds or get an illness from one day of unhealthy choices. However, in that same note, one day of healthy meals will not undo a lifetime of bad choices. But choosing a piece of fruit over the pastry every morning will, over time, lead to a healthier body, a lower weight, and a more energetic self. It is our job to be persistent and to keep working on our self-efficacy. If I want to become a better writer, the best thing I can do is write every day. Whether it is a lengthy document or just a few sentences, the practice of writing will help my words flow better. And if I tell myself every day that I am a writer, eventually I will believe it (as we discussed earlier about reframing our thoughts). We must be persistent to persevere.

6. **Remember that success does not happen overnight.** Similar to the tip above about perseverance, it is important to remember that Rome was not built in one day and success is not something that occurs overnight. A person does not wake up one day and run 26.2 miles or graduate as a doctor. A business is not built in a matter of hours, but rather over weeks, months, and years, with blood, sweat, and tears. Remind yourself of your past successes and how long it took to achieve them. And ask other people how they accomplished their goals. Whether or not you also share the same dream as they do, it can be a great lesson on how our dreams can take hard work and time. For instance, law school takes three years typically, but most people have their undergraduate degree already. Thus, if someone's dream is to become a lawyer, they will be in school for approximately seven years. And after they have earned two degrees, they still cannot practice law. The person will need to take the State Bar Exam to become a licensed attorney in his or her state. No matter what your dream is, it is important to remember that success takes time and effort, even if it looks effortless.

7. **Set reasonable expectations for you.** If you struggled in the past to simply earn a C on your papers, it is important not to go into your next English class assuming you will either fail the class or get an A easily. While either could happen, it would be better for you to focus on making your C papers become a B, and then your B papers into an A. Instead of going in with too high or too low of an expectation, make small, reasonable goals to improve your work day-by-day, semester-by-semester.

8. **Acknowledge your successes.** Celebrate submitting an essay or completing a homework assignment. It can be easy to focus on the fact that you still have more tasks left to accomplish – whether it is for the semester or just in general – but by taking time to celebrate your small wins, you will be reminded of your successes. NOTE: You can also help improve other people's self-efficacy by noting what they did well and acknowledging their successes. For example, you could tell a friend that you are not only proud of them for submitting their essay, but that they did an awesome job on it as well.

9. **Actually do the work.** While our mindset obviously plays a key role in our success, it is not enough to simply believe we will be successful. It is still essential to do the work. People with a higher sense of self-efficacy tend to put in more work to succeed at their task than those who have a lower sense of self-efficacy. After all, our essay will not write itself, but if we do not submit one, it could lower our grade and thus reduce our self-efficacy.

10. **Surround yourself with people who believe in your success and encourage you to chase your wildest dreams.** There are a couple of statistics that state that we are the average of the five or eight people we spend the most time with. Whether those statistics are accurate or not, the truth is that the people who we spend time with do influence us. If your spouse stops eating meat, you will likely stop eating meat for at least a few meals (such as when you go to a vegan café or when your partner makes a dish without any meat). Or if your best friend drops a class you were going to take together, it could be tempting to do the same and take the class another semester when you can take it together. By surrounding yourself with people who believe in you and encourage you not to quit, your self-doubt can easily be squashed thanks to their verbal affirmations and social persuasion.

Missy's Memoir

{Do you believe in your ability to succeed at a task or an assignment? What about at any or every task or assignment? The moment you find something where you doubt yourself, that is when we need to work on your self-efficacy.}

Missy has always believed that she is a weak writer. After failing a paper, she had worked hard on in sixth grade, she has come to terms with the fact that she is *just not a writer.* In her English class this semester, however, her professor has told her class that they cannot use terms like *I cannot do this,* or *I suck at that,* when it comes to describing their ability to write. In class recently, everyone had to work in small groups on revising each of their "working thesis statements" for an upcoming essay.

"I'm so frustrated by this," Missy admitted to her friend, classmate, and roommate, Kaley. "I do not know how to say that I can do this when I simply feel like I cannot."

"It is a mindset," Kaley reminded her friend. "You need to work on why you feel this way."

"Do you feel this way?" Missy inquired. "It feels like most of us struggle with classes like math or writing. I am a numbers person, so words do not benefit my skill set."

"That. That right there is your issue. Your attitude means you come into class already believing that you cannot be successful. You have a thinking problem, not a writing problem, and the sooner you realize that the more successful you will be," Brody chimed in.

Missy paused for a minute, unable to argue with her friends, but then realized she had no argument. She admitted, "I have been working on reframing how I feel about writing, but I still feel I have not gotten to the core of it."

"How so?" Her professor inquired when coming to check in on the small group work.

"Well, I have never felt like a writer, and even when I say I can write, it just feels disingenuous."

"Why do you feel you cannot write?"

"Because I always fail my essays and English classes," Missy began. "It feels like I was born to understand numbers and not words."

"Well," her professor added. "What was your grade on our last essay?"

"A B+," Missy stated.

"Wow, that is amazing, Miss," Rowdy cheered her on.

"You are absolutely right, Rowdy. And how long did you work on it, Missy?" their professor asked.

"The truth?" Missy asked reluctantly. "I pulled an all-nighter."

"You did a paper in one night that earned you a B+. Imagine if you had done it over one week or one month. Now, really think about when you first started struggling with the idea that you are not a writer. When was it?"

Missy pondered for a moment on her prior English classes, wondering when she determined that she simply could not write. "It was in sixth grade," she finally admitted. "I worked hard on a paper and failed it and decided that I clearly was a poor writer."

"And from then until now you have reaffirmed that idea every day, convincing yourself that you cannot write, allowing fear to help you focus on anything besides our class, being apprehensive, and believing that you do not belong in our classroom," her professor explained. "But do you write, Missy?"

"I like poetry," Missy admitted. "And I do write poems pretty frequently. I just suck at academic writing."

"Let's reframe that," her professor stated.

"You're right," Missy admitted. "I like writing poetry and I am working on improving my scholarly writing. And you are absolutely right, Kaley," she agreed after thinking about their words. "But what can I do about it?"

"Change your attitude, change your life," Kaley responded with a smile. "Now let us revise these working thesis statements."

"No, let us revise these amazing thesis statements to make them even stronger," Brody reframed Kaley's words. "And let us start with a very strong one. Missy, let us look at yours."

Workbook Questions

1. Why is it important for both Missy and her professor to understand the basis for her low self-efficacy and why she believes she cannot succeed in her college composition class? Explain.

2. What can her friends, family, or even her professors do to help her reframe her low self-efficacy? How do her friends and her instructor help in this story? Explain.

Kaley's Quiz

1. Self-efficacy is our mindset and only we can influence it or change it.
   True
   (False)

2. We either have high or low self-efficacy. No one can have both at the same time.
   True
   (False)

3. Confidence and self-esteem are related to self-efficacy. While they are all similar, each of them is still unique in and of itself.
   (True)
   False

4. We should reframe our thoughts, words, and actions to improve our self-efficacy.
   (True)
   False

5. Albert Bandura said there are five sources for our self-efficacy.
   True
   (False)

Brody's Breakdown

- We all struggle with self-efficacy in some area of our personal and/or professional life. It is due to our belief in our ability to succeed, built upon our past successes and failures, what we have been told by others, and what we have told ourselves.
- We need to reframe our self-efficacy by rephrasing what we say to ourselves and about ourselves.
- It is important to be aware that while self-efficacy impacts just us, how we talk to and treat others can potentially impact their self-efficacy as well. Be mindful and aware of your word choices, thoughts, and opinions so that you do not cause other people to have lower self-efficacy. And on that same note, be sure not to allow someone else's negative belief to change your choices and lower your self-efficacy.

CHAPTER 3
FEELING LIKE A FRAUD: UNDERSTANDING IMPOSTER SYNDROME

{Have you ever felt like a fraud? Then you have experienced imposter syndrome.}

© fizkes/Shutterstock.com

Rowdy's Rule: *Imposter syndrome occurs when you believe you do not belong in the room. While it can feel isolating and as if you are the only one who feels this way, the irony is that it impacts everyone. No matter how qualified you are to be in said room, anyone and everyone can experience feeling like a fraud, like an imposter, and as if they are about to be unmasked.*

Most of us have felt the effects of imposter syndrome at some point in our lives. A world-renowned doctor may feel like a fraud when they go into work. A business owner may worry that their customer will realize that they are not capable of running a business. And a student may fear that they do not belong in the class. Many students actually fear being in class, concerned that they are not capable enough when it comes to the class requirements. I have heard graduate students worry about writing their thesis or dissertation in two or three years. And I have had undergraduate students worry about their ability to write an essay for our class. But the truth is we write daily – whether it is a text message, social media post, email, or even in the form of journaling or creative writing. So why is it that we suddenly fear the act of writing, something we do every day?

Imposter syndrome is a feeling that makes us believe that we do not belong. Its irony is that something that can make us feel so isolated (how often have you ever felt someone else does not belong in the room?) is actually so common. We all have times where we believe we do not belong. We think that it was luck, a fluke, or a mistake that allowed us into this room, never thinking to ourselves that we are in said room because we do belong. But the thing about imposter syndrome is that none of it is a fact; it is simply a feeling. After all it is our *belief* that we do not belong. It is our *thought* that we should not be in the room. It is not a fact, but rather a work of fiction that we have created in our minds. And personally, when I write fiction, I would prefer to write an engaging best seller than one that makes me doubt my own belonging. Do you not feel the same way?

This is where our confidence, self-efficacy, and imposter syndrome come into play. The same way that a well-educated, experienced, and successful doctor may doubt their ability and worry that someone is going to unmask their true self – a fake who is terrible at medicine – we can fear the things we do every day. Our imposter syndrome can make us feel like we do not have the knowledge necessary to do our job, and it can be so bad that we do not even think we suffer from this condition. Imposter syndrome can hinder our ability to succeed in class, at work, and in life. The ways to work on getting past this are similar to increasing our self-efficacy, and just like with self-efficacy and self-confidence, it is something we need to work on every day.

10 Ways to Get Over Imposter Syndrome

© G-Stock Studio/Shutterstock.com

{Even if it does not always feel like it, you do belong in whatever room you are in. You are not a fraud. And spoiler alert - almost everyone else in the room with you likely feels the same exact way. But we all belong.}

1. **Recognize your education, experience, and success.** A doctor who feels like a fraud should remember that he or she went to medical school and learned how to practice medicine. Similarly, students should realize that they have completed the necessary prerequisites required for their college to admit them into their class, and thus are capable of succeeding.

2. **Remember the things you have done well with a daily *confidence practice*.** Some people like to keep a box or binder full of their accomplishments. Others prefer to hang up their degrees, medals, awards, and trophies. But another thing you can do is adopt a *confidence practice*. It is a term I coined for strengthening our self-efficacy through a daily practice that focuses on our self-efficacy and confidence. Similar to a gratitude or meditation practice, take a few minutes each day to remember or write down your successes. Whenever you feel like an imposter, you can meditate on your accomplishments and remember all the things you have done well. This way, even if you are traveling and away from said box or binder, you can still find a way to work on improving your imposter syndrome.

3. **Remember that comparison is the thief of joy.** We are each unique and have our own path to success, happiness, and life. If you compare yourself to someone else, you will always fall short. The truth is there is someone who is better at something than us and someone who struggles with the same thing more than we do. Someone might be incredibly talented at something and may find they have a lack of success at something you are talented at. The only person who you should ever compare yourself to is you. Strive to be better than you were yesterday. Work on creating a stronger essay than your last paper. Your past self is the only person you should compare yourself to. If not, you will always feel like an imposter because you will be attempting to be someone who you simply are not.

4. **Mistakes and failures do not make you a fraud or an imposter.** The best thing about being human is that we will all make mistakes. Every single person has made a mistake. Whether it is your idol, a rock star, a successful athlete, or someone who is succeeding at your dream, they have failed. They have made mistakes. The goal, however, is to learn from our failures. Remember, the American actress Mae West said it best: "To err is human." Mistakes will happen, we will fail sometimes, and that is okay.

5. **Avoid perfectionism.** This goes along with the last point on failure. I consider myself to be a recovering perfectionist. When I was a kid, I would write down notes in class, go home, and rewrite them so they were color-coded and in perfect penmanship. Any time I made a mistake and needed to scratch something out, I threw out what I had done and started over from scratch. I wanted what I wrote to be perfect, but all it turned out to be was an epic waste of time. I did not get an A for having the prettiest notes. While trying to improve yourself, your skills, and your abilities is an important goal, trying to be perfect is simply going to feed into the idea that you are an imposter. After all, none of us are perfect, and expecting ourselves to be is simply going to be a goal we fail at.

6. **Call it what it is – imposter syndrome – and recognize that you belong here just as much as everyone else.** When we are able to address something as what it is, it loses some of its power. Recognize imposter syndrome for what it is: a feeling. Everyone feels like an imposter at times and wonders if they belong in the room you are in, and the truth is, you all belong in that room. We all belong in any room we want to be in.

7. **Fake it until you make it.** Just as this technique can help with our confidence, it can also help with imposter syndrome. Sometimes just winging it and telling yourself and everyone else that you can do it will help. In fact, in an NBCNews article, Dr. Isha Gupta, a neurologist from IGEA Brain and Spine, shared that the mere act of smiling will create a chemical reaction in your brain and release hormones such as dopamine (to increase happiness) and serotonin (**to lower stress**) (Spector 2018). Thus, the mere act of smiling when you are sad can actually make your brain happier. Using that same concept of tricking your brain into being happier, you can also trick your brain into feeling like you are not an imposter, even if you do feel like a fraud. And do not ever forget that Steve Jobs once said, "The people who are crazy enough to think they can change the world are the ones who do." So fake it until you make it, make the impossible possible, and trick your brain into believing you are the best. After a while, your brain will stop being tricked and believe it to be nothing other than the truth.

8. **Nobody knows what he or she is doing and everyone feels like a fraud.** This is the most isolating aspect of imposter syndrome. We all feel like a fraud, but we do not realize everyone else does as well. The truth is there is no manual for life or how our life path should look. We are all simply winging this little thing called life.

9. **Be kind to yourself.** A common idea is that we do not always treat ourselves the way we would treat our best friend, or even a complete stranger, but that we should. It somehow seems more normalized to be mean and demand more from ourselves than what we would expect someone else to demand of themselves. Imposter syndrome is, in and of itself, a mean voice in our heads that tells us we are not enough. This negative self-talk simply ups our anxiety, lowers our self-esteem and self-confidence, and increases our stress levels. Instead, we need to focus on being kinder to ourselves. Treat yourself the way you would treat your best friend. Talk to yourself using positive affirmations. And remember that everyone makes mistakes, has failures, and we are all perfectly imperfect people.

10. **Remember that it is only a feeling.** Imposter syndrome is what happens when we feel like our win was just a stroke of luck or we feel that we do not have what it takes to do something. It is not a fact; it is just a feeling. It can help to tell yourself that it is just a feeling - "I feel getting an A on my essay was just lucky" – instead of saying that luck was the reason you got an A on your essay. By recognizing that it is a feeling you create a distance between the feeling and the facts. Because at the end of the day, imposter syndrome is not the truth. Rather it is simply your emotions that make you feel as if you are a fraud.

Missy's Memoir

{If you feel as if you do not belong where you are today (at work, in school, or simply just in general), where do you think you belong?}

Missy comes home from work one day very excited to tell her best friend her good news.

"Guess what?" She gushes to Kaley.

"What happened at work?" Kaley asks.

"So my boss called me into her office this afternoon. I was a little worried at first, but," Missy pauses to add suspense to her story. "She told me I got the job I applied for a couple months ago! I am officially the store manager, and my boss is going to a bigger store nearby to be the store manager there," she beams.

"Miss, that is amazing!" Kaley responds excitedly. "I am so proud of you. What does this mean besides the new title? We must celebrate!"

"Basically, less sales and more of a general overview of the store, a big pay raise, a new title, and I get to be the boss. Can you believe it? I do not know how I got this. I must have tricked them into thinking I was actually store manager material," Missy says, half chuckling, but half being serious.

"What do you mean?" Kaley asks, immediately observing the slight fear and doubt in Missy's voice.

"I mean, come on, Kaley. We both know I am not store manager material. I know that, you know that, even my soon-to-be former boss knows that. I must have convinced them to hire me somehow. I just do not know how," Missy explains. "Maybe it was magic?" She laughs at her question, still pondering what else could have made her manager choose her to be the new head of their store.

"Miss," Kaley begins. "You have been there for three years. You work full-time while juggling school. You have the track record for the most sales nearly every month. And you make sure the women who try on the beautiful clothes at your store feel pretty and sparkly inside. That is a gift not everyone possesses. Who would make a better store manager than you?"

Missy smiles and is clearly touched by her friend's kind words. "Kay, you are so sweet. But you are my friend. Of course you are saying this. But all my coworkers are amazing. Anyone of them would likely make a better store manager than me."

"I do not get how you can spend 30 minutes just on your face every morning," Kaley tells Missy. She is referring to Missy's intense, ten-step skincare routine that she religiously follows. Twice a day you can find her near her bathroom sink, cleansing, exfoliating, and moisturizing her skin with the trendiest serums and sheet masks available. She started this routine as a teenager when her skin first started breaking out, and she has made it her morning and nightly ritual ever since then. "I mean I wake up early, but it is to get to Pilates and finish my workout for the day."

"It is just something I am used to," Missy tells her friend. "Just like you would feel off all day if you missed your workout, my skin feels off when I skip a step. But I do not understand how the topic changed."

Kaley then asks Missy if she puts in this type of effort when it comes to her self-efficacy and confidence with work.

"What do you mean?" Missy asks.

"I mean, you wake up early to focus on your skincare regimen, but it does not feel like work because you have done it for years now. But do you put in that type of daily effort when it comes to simply believing in yourself?"

"Do you mean do I tell myself every day that I can and will be successful at my job?" Missy inquires.

"Yeah," Kaley states. "Authentic confidence comes from within. We have to work on that daily. Do you? I spend time every day telling myself I can and will be successful at anything I want

{While we may all fear something, would you rather hide under the covers or face your fears?}

Rowdy's Rule: *The one thing that connects low confidence, low self-efficacy, and imposter syndrome together is fear. The greatest freedom and the strongest growth occur when we overcome our fear and chase after our dreams.*

Suzy Kassem's quote, "Doubt kills more dreams than failure ever will," has always been a gentle reminder to me that I need to face my fears. The truth is we all have fears. And while it is easier to tell someone that we need to face our fears than it is to actually face them, Kassem's words are true: our doubt, or fear, in our abilities will destroy our dreams far more so than failure ever will.

I cannot do this. How often have you thought these words? Whether it is writing a paper for class, starting a business, or becoming fluent in another language, there is almost always something in this world that scares us. We fear failure, making that the number one belief in our minds. After all, if I never try to do something, I can never fail at it.

But I want us to view this from a new lens for a minute. If I never try to write my paper for class, sure, I cannot fail it in the sense that my words cannot be critiqued or criticized. My words, however, also cannot be praised or given feedback on ways to be developed over the course of the semester or our lifetime. And if we really consider this, if I never write the paper, does that not just mean I am going to automatically fail anyways? Perhaps my words are never edited by my professor's red pen, but that is only because they are never written down.

It is far easier to not do something than it is to try and possibly fail in the process. If I never try to start my own nonprofit, it can never be unsuccessful. Perhaps I do not succeed in creating it or I build it and find that it eventually falls apart. If I never start my nonprofit, there is no way for it to ever fail. If I never start my business, there is no way for it to go bankrupt or become an investment loss. But by never starting that company I have dreamt of in my dreams since I was nine, I would argue I am failing even more. I am failing myself, both the nine-year-old version and the woman I am today. I am failing the dream I have had for decades by not even trying to make it come true. And by fearing that essay that is due on Monday, I can choose to ignore it and automatically fail, or I can choose to try to write the best paper I can, get feedback on it, learn from it, and know that even if my paper did not get a passing grade, at least I did everything I could to try.

The opposite of failing is not passing, in my opinion; it is trying. And this is where self-efficacy comes into play.

Many of us struggle with writing. I have had students tell me that they wrote a paper that they did not submit because they were concerned it was not "good enough". Or that they began working on an essay, but felt they could not finish it, so they stopped trying. Every time I hear a story like this, it breaks my heart. The truth is that even a paper that earns a low grade will be far more beneficial than a paper that is never submitted. Aside from the fact that 50% is still higher than 0%, a paper that is submitted leaves room for growth and knowledge. The writer can get feedback and learn from their work on what they can do to improve their next paper or possibly revise the current one.

Doing something new can often be scary. After all, we do not have a "thesis," aka our GPS or roadmap for our paper, to help guide us on how to get to our destination. Whether your dream is to start a business, become a star athlete, win an Oscar, or graduate from college, it can be scary to try to do so when you have never done it before. It can also be scarier if no one you know has already accomplished this. After all, if your mother won an Oscar or your father began a successful company, you have someone you can reach out to and seek advice from.

Arguably, the number one thing for success would be taking on a mindset of fearlessness. A lack of confidence is rooted in fear. It is our *fear from previously failing* that often makes us believe we cannot be successful this time around. Low self-efficacy is rooted in fear. It is our *fear of failing* that makes us believe we cannot be successful. And imposter syndrome is rooted in fear. It is our *fear that we are failing* that leads us to believe we do not belong in the room. It is up to us to not only cultivate our confidence, increase our self-efficacy, and recognize that our imposter syndrome is a feeling and not a fact, but also to focus on creating a mindset based on fearlessness. And it is our job to avoid letting fear stop us from pursuing our wildest dreams. Whether you try and fail or you avoid trying altogether, the end result is the same: failure. At least when you try, you have the chance of succeeding and can learn from your mistakes, if you need to try again.

Fear can hold us back from trying, but by not even trying, we are automatically failing. But by trying, we understand the importance of not letting our self-apprehensiveness or low self-efficacy keep us from at least making an attempt. By trying, we are slowly changing our self-efficacy, and as we will discuss, changing our belief system. Bandura defined self-efficacy as our internal feeling of whether or not we will succeed at something, and this covers a variety of tasks. Whether it is imagining the idea of changing your career you have spent a decade working on, or moving to another country by yourself, we all are apprehensive about something. But by changing that idea, removing the fear, removing the apprehension, research shows that we are far more likely to succeed.

10 Ways to Get Over Your Fear of Writing

{Will fear prevent you from ever starting?}

1. **Avoid procrastinating.** Procrastination is not just the thief of time. It can also cause us to stress out and become more anxious. After all, every minute, hour, day, or week that we choose not to work on our assignment, we continue to worry about it and keep it in the back of our minds. Think about the last time you procrastinated on an assignment (whether it was for school, work, or a personal task). How did it make you feel? Stressed out or relaxed? Anxious or calm? Chances are you did not feel the latter.

2. **Do not fear constructive criticism.** Constructive feedback is one of the kindest things we can give one another. Without it, we are left without any ideas on ways to strengthen what we have already done. And if you still feel that constructive feedback makes you feel nervous or anxious, think about it in a new way. If what you wrote was so perfect that there was absolutely nothing you could do to improve it, are you actually learning anything from this assignment? And if you are not learning anything from this assignment, then what is the point of doing it? Spoiler Alert: There is no such thing as a perfect paper because even the best written paper will have room to improve, the same way even the most off-topic essay will have done something great. But this leads us to the next tip.

3. **Forget perfection.** There is no such thing as a perfect paper. The truth is that the editorial process is never over. We can write the strongest paper ever, and still, a year later, we will likely want to revise it and reword it slightly. If we equate perfection with success, we will spend our entire life failing and never learning from these failures.

4. **Utilize baby steps.** If you break up an essay into a paragraph a day, you can write and revise a strong paper in just a week or two. Instead of trying to do an entire paper in one night (the famous all-nighter almost all of us have experienced at some point or another), it is better for your mental health and sleep schedule to break down your tasks into small, easy-to-complete steps.

5. **Seek support from everyone.** Whether it is reading your essay out loud to your mom, asking your best friend to help you strengthen your thesis statement, reaching out to a tutor for help with editing your paper, or contacting your instructor for clarifications on the essay prompt, the best way to reduce your fear of writing is to strengthen your understanding of the assignment.

6. **Find others who have experienced similar fears.** Similar to the advice above about seeking support from everyone around you, seek out others who could have similar fears as you. Perhaps your older brother or sister failed a class and understands your fear of failing. They might be able to ease your concerns and help you learn ways to improve your success in school, as well as show you that even though he or she failed one class, they still graduated (perhaps even with honors) from college. By knowing others who have experienced similar fears as you, whether these are current fears or ones in the past, you can see how life will continue or at least recognize that you are not the only one who feels this way.

7. **Figure out the reason why you feel fearful.** It is very easy to simply state that I am nervous to write a research paper. However, the more important question to ask myself is why?

Why do I fear this essay? Do I fear other types of essays? Perhaps I am nervous to write a research paper because I have never done so before. It can be scary to write an essay in a new style, but by being aware of why I feel this fear, I can address and overcome it. For example, I can read about how to write a research paper online or within a textbook that has been assigned to our class. I can also work with my professor, a tutor, or even a study group with my classmates. By slowly learning more about this type of essay, I can remove the mystery surrounding it and focus on strengthening my knowledge when it comes to it.

8. **Recognize that a challenging class or an assignment does not equate to a failure.** I love to challenge students in my class. I always tell them that they will earn their A, and that an assignment should not be easy, but rather it should be challenging. I explain to them that the reason is because an easy assignment might be nice in the moment (it is quick to complete and an automatic A), but it will not teach us anything we do not already know. A challenging assignment, on the other hand, might not be something we want to do in the moment (it is time consuming and requires us to work hard for that A), but it will teach us something we did not know before. A fear-based mindset views difficult classes and assignments as threats to their existence and success. But a fearless mindset allows us to view these challenges as ways to improve our knowledge and understanding, thus creating the foundation for our success.

9. **Remember that we all have different ideas of what constitutes as failure.** While someone may fear not passing a class, someone else may fear not getting an A in the same class. Our definition of failure can vary between what class or assignment we are focused on, as well as from person to person. When I was young, I felt a B stood for "Bad," and anything less than a 90% was subpar on my end. However, I had peers who simply wanted to get a C, pass the class, and never think about the subject again. As I got older, I felt anything besides an A in my English classes (my major) was a failure for me. Yet so many of my classmates simply wanted to complete their general education requirement and avoid any other class that required us to write a paper. The truth is, it is relative based on who you are and what your goals are at that point in time. It is important to remember that your idea of failure might be a win for someone else. Perhaps even registering for a class scares someone. Then, the fact that you are in the class, even if you are nervous you might fail it, is a win from their perspective. Success comes in all forms, and it is important to celebrate the things you do that might seem fearless and like a success to someone else.

10. **Know your self-worth.** It is essential in all aspects of our life to know our self-worth, and, as the quote says, we all need to, "Know your worth. Then add tax." The truth is we will all fail at something. Perhaps it is a class, a paper, a project, a dream, but whatever it is, the best thing we can do is to learn from our failure. Without it, we would never learn anything new. However, a person who has low self-worth will equate this failure to mean they themselves are a failure. But you must remember that you are so much more than your class, paper, project, dream, or whatever else it might be. Even if you fail the first time, that does

not mean you are a failure. In fact, with that mindset, Thomas Edison, who invented the light bulb, would be considered a failure instead of the innovative and incredible inventor we view him as. It took him over a thousand tries to make the light bulb a reality. When he was asked how it felt to fail that many times, he replied, "I didn't fail a thousand times. The light bulb was an invention with a thousand steps." If Edison viewed his first step for inventing the light bulb as a failure, we may still only have light from candles and the sun. And if that quote from Edison did not resonate with you enough to believe it, he also stated, "I have not failed. I've just found 10,000 ways that won't work." Remember, you are not your failures. Failures can help you get to the next step. And if all else fails, simply remember: I am enough. Because you are enough, no matter how you do on a paper or in a class.

Missy's Memoir

{Does fear hold you back from chasing your wildest dreams? If so, is failure truly less scary than living a life where you never tried to make your dreams into your reality?}

Missy and her crew, Rowdy, Brody, and Kaley, decide to go out to dinner. At the Thai restaurant, the four friends order a feast with various curries, appetizers, and Thai iced teas and coffees for all.

"How are you all doing?" Kaley asks between sips of her sweet tea. "I feel as if we have not been together in ages."

"It has been a busy semester," Rowdy responds. "I have such a heavy course load since I am taking more units than what is required from a full-time student."

"I get it," Brody responds as he picks up a spring roll to dip in the peanut sauce. "I have a great job, but it has kept me busy. I feel as if I spend all morning and afternoon at school, all afternoon and evening at work, and I have to eat, sleep, relax, and do my homework at night. I obviously cannot do everything, so I keep skipping my sleep, which is not at all healthy."

The three notice that Missy has been rather quiet. She stares down at her iced tea as she slowly sips it, avoiding eye contact with her friends.

"Miss," Kaley asks. "You are rather quiet today. What is going on?"

"Yeah, Miss, how are you?" Rowdy adds.

"Everything is good," Missy says.

After a minute of silence though, Brody adds, "And?"

"And I am glad we could do this," she says.

"Missy, we are your best friends. You do not seem fine. What is going on?" Rowdy states.

Missy looks at them and finally sighs, realizing her friends can tell when she is not being honest.

"Okay," she says, putting her almost empty drink down on the table. "I am scared." She takes a breath while her friends try to think about what might be scaring her. "I think I am just not cut out for college. I think I am going to fail two of my classes, I am struggling to juggle work and school, and I had my paper critiqued in class three days ago. Everyone told me I had a weak thesis statement, no conclusion, and not nearly enough analysis. I just cannot do this anymore. It was almost better when I did not waste everyone's time with my first essay. It was truly awful so I never even submitted it. Now the whole class knows why." Missy looks at her friends and it is clear she is exhausted, but also that a weight has been lifted off her shoulders.

"Thank you for sharing," Kaley says before she hugs her friend. "Missy, you are scared, but so are we." Rowdy and Brody nod in unison. "So let us look at each issue you mentioned. First, I constantly worry I am not cut out for college. I am scared I will fail a class or not succeed. But I think we all fear that feeling of not belonging or being an imposter, you know?"

"Yeah," Brody adds. "Juggling work and school is hard. I do not even know how I do it some days," he chuckles. "But we just take it day-by-day and focus on time management. I have found that by not procrastinating, it really helps me reduce my anxiety and stress."

Rowdy smiles at Missy and adds, "I get it. I am taking so many units this semester and have noticed my work is not at the same caliber that I am used to doing. When I began working on my last paper, I felt it was so horrible. But I realized that getting even partial credit was better than a zero. Plus, I figure that even a really off-topic paper will give me feedback that helps me improve my next paper. That is a good thing!"

Brody adds, "You are also focusing on the things you are struggling with right now, but when we study, you only focus on the subject you are good at and avoid the one you likely need to focus on. Why do you think that is?"

Missy looks at her friends, unsure of how to respond at first. "You are right, Brody," Missy admits. "I think I do not want to write the paper and spend time on something I know I will fail."

"How do you know you will fail it?" Brody asks.

"Because I always fail essays," Missy states. "Why waste time studying for a subject I know I will fail?"

"Then why did we enroll in this class?" Kaley asks her roommate.

"It is a requirement for our degree," Missy responds.

Brody asks Missy, "So if you have to take the class, but you do not study for it, how exactly do you plan to be successful?"

"You are right, Brody. It is rooted in my fear of failure, which ironically will only let me fail," Missy admits.

Kaley adds, "And I was at the feedback in class, Miss. Sure you are remembering what they told you to do to improve your writing, but do you remember what they said you did well?"

Missy looks at Kaley and answers, "I think that I had a good title, a captivating hook, and that I used really strong quotes that left the reader wanting to know more about each text."

"Exactly!" Kaley replies. "Missy, you did a great job. And you earned a B on that paper. A B does not stand for *bad*, it stands for above average, or as I prefer to say, beautiful. Because it is a beautiful grade."

Missy smiles. "You guys are the best. Thank you for these important reminders."

"Of course," Rowdy says. "It actually helps a lot to know others have or are experiencing these same situations or feelings as we are."

"Just remember that we love you, Miss. And you belong in the classroom, the boardroom, or any room you want to be in just as much as anyone else," Kaley states.

"Thank you," Missy beams. "You are all correct. I can do this. Just take it day-by-day, right, Brody?" Brody nods his head in agreement. "Okay, now enough talk about school and these fears. I want to hear about everyone's plans for break and to dig into this peanut curry, though maybe not in that order," he laughs.

"That works for me," Kaley says. "The Pad Thai is calling my name."

The four friends begin to eat their meal together while catching up on their plans over break and feeling comforted knowing that their fears are normal and that they are not alone.

Workbook Questions

1. What can Missy and her friends do to help ease these fears they face every day? What are they doing that could be helping them? And why do you say that it is helping them manage their fear and make their mindset fearless instead?
2. How and why does the fear of failure make Missy nervous for her English class? Additionally, has the fear of failure ever made you consider not completing an assignment instead of trying and possibly failing? Why?

Kaley's Quiz

1. Fear does not connect confidence, low self-efficacy, and imposter syndrome.
   True
   (False)

2. Procrastination can help increase our fear, anxiety, stress, and nervousness.
   (True)
   False

3. Seeking support from others can possibly help you, but it will not reduce any fear you might feel.
   True
   (False)

4. Perfectionism is a good thing that we should strive for. If we write a perfect paper, we will earn a perfect score on it, and if we have an A in our class or on our assignment, we will no longer fear failure since we are not failing.
   True
   (False)

5. Everyone will fail at something or at some point in his or her life.
   (True)
   False

CHAPTER 5
IMPACTING SOMEONE ELSE'S
SELF-EFFICACY

{While we can change our own self-efficacy, other people also influence it and we influence other people's belief system and mindsets as well.}

Rowdy's Rule: *We are influenced by other people and we also influence other people's beliefs in their own ability to succeed. Since confidence and high self-efficacy are a superpower of sorts, it is our job to recognize that we now have a great responsibility to bear as Stan Lee's protagonist, Peter Parker, said: "With great power comes great responsibility."*

Motivational speaker Jim Rohn famously stated that "[we] are the average of the five people [we] spend the most with." But at the end of the day, it is up to each of us to determine how we feel about our ability to succeed at a given task. Sure, seeing other people – like my teachers –

tell me that I can write well has boosted my confidence levels and my self-efficacy. But what if they had not liked my writing? Would that have made me a weak writer? Should that have changed the course of my life? Should I have studied another subject in school or had a different career? You are likely shaking your head no right now. However, our teachers are not the only reason we follow our path. Sure, they help us along the way, but we choose our own path because it brings us joy. I chose my path the same way each of us chooses our own, and even if I had teachers who had hated my writing, this would not have deterred me. This is because I went into school already having a strong self-efficacy and love of writing.

We likely have been influenced to feel the fear we feel for certain tasks, subjects, and assignments throughout our life by those around us. Our parents, our friends, and our teachers can influence us for either the better or the worse. Think back to a subject you feel apprehensive about. Did someone else agree with your concern that it was not your strong suit? Did this get you to begin feeling that they had validated your worry? When I was younger, I doubted my own mathematical abilities, but I also dealt with others doubting my math capabilities. It brought down my belief in my own ability to succeed because I already did not believe in myself. Whereas with writing, this was impossible since I would never have given anyone else's belief enough value to deter my own. We doubt our own ability when it is something rooted in our fear of failure.

Self-efficacy is about you and your belief in your ability to succeed at a given task, such as writing. But who all determine it? It is easy to believe we are the only ones who impact our self-efficacy. But our teachers, our parents, our family, our friends all have an impact on how we perceive ourselves. Think about it like this: if you grew up with your parents, your friends, your coaches, and everyone around you telling you that you were an amazing track athlete or a star basketball player, you likely have always thought of yourself as being great at that sport. The same goes with if you were told you had an entrepreneurial mindset - you likely have considered or already run a small business. If everyone you knew praised your writing, you likely are reading this book knowing that you are a strong writer already. But in that same way, if you were always told you were not good at something or that you struggled with it, you have likely carried that fear into your life today.

For example, growing up I believed I was the worst runner. I could barely run down the block. When I had to run a mile in school, I would always come in last, and finally, by 15, I gave up on even finishing the mandatory mile in my physical education class. I was a sophomore in high school at the time, and as I ran, I felt my stomach cramp up, my legs want to give up, and the sun hitting my face just made me worry about sunspots and wrinkles in the future. I ran around the track twice, taking longer than some of the runners took to run the entire four laps. But I forgot in that moment how many others were going at a slower pace along with me. I would alternate between walking, sprinting, and slowly jogging, before I finally said I quit. I never expected that less than a year later, I would fall in love with the sport.

Quitting that mandatory mile just reminded me of how much I was not a runner. *A runner would not quit, after all,* I argued in my mind. But what I forgot were all the things that made me quit; and it was far more than cramps, weak legs, and the hot sunny day. I quit because I had conditioned myself into believing I could not do this. And because of my mindset, I proved myself correct. Sure, I did not finish running the mile on that warm day in May, but did that mean I was not a runner? By my definition, it did. However, I learned years later that the only person who is a runner is one who calls themselves that and the same is true for a non-runner. And six years after I quit that mile as a sophomore in high school, I ran a marathon. No one ever asks me how long it took me to run 26.2 miles or how many marathons I have run since then; they simply call me a runner because I tell them I am one.

I was 21 when I ran that marathon, and I am proud to say that even though there were men in their seventies running faster than me, I still finished. At mile 20 I was told by one of the locals cheering us on, that there was a 78-year-old man ahead of me. Even though this stranger was nearly 60 years my senior, he had run a marathon the previous day, gotten on a plane that evening, flown across the country, and he was still ahead of me. It is a great way to think of life though. So often there are going to be people who are stronger at something or more successful than we are. This is not a bad thing. We should cheer them on, support them, and empower them, while not giving up on our own dreams. After all, as I shared earlier, all most people care about is that I ran a marathon. No one cares about my time or who was ahead of me or behind me. Remember when you are writing an essay that all people look for is that you wrote a strong essay. Maybe someone else will write a stronger essay in your mind, but if you write the strongest paper you can, is that not all that truly matters?

Most people will not tell you that "you suck at tennis" or "you are terrible at biology" or "you are the worst amateur astronomer." People know that saying something like this would be mean, make them unpopular, and is just unnecessary and untrue. Rather, you are more likely to hear something such as "math just is not your subject like art is" or "you gave me a huge nose in your portrait sketch. You might want to work on perfecting your nose drawing skills." These comments are not kind, but they might be accurate. Perhaps I am better at art than I am at math, or maybe I can draw someone's eyes well, but their nose always has been a challenge. Even though they are being honest (as seen with the latter comment) or trying to tell you that you are good at something (with the former one), you are likely left remembering that math and drawing noses are not your forte. Other people can also impact your self-efficacy when you get constructive criticism. While we have discussed why feedback is so essential for our growth and learning, that does not mean it might not make us feel bad. It is our job to recognize that feedback such as, "your thesis felt a bit weak since it did not act as a roadmap, or GPS, for the rest of the essay," is for our benefit. It is also our choice to recognize that feedback, such as the one about our drawing, can be used as constructive feedback if we ask ourselves, how can I improve the nose? And it is our choice to view a comment such as the one about our math skills versus our artistic skills in one of two ways: either it is that we are not good at math or it is that we are artists. The latter will help our confidence, self-efficacy, and self-worth far more than the former will. And if you want to be a mathematician and an artist, no one can ever stop you. Remember, you get to define who you are. So, are you the artist, the mathematician, or both?

The truth is that we all impact the self-efficacy of everyone around us. If my parents had raised me to believe I was a horrible writer, I probably would never have written this book. If my teachers had built up my confidence when it came to numbers, maybe I would have become a math professor instead. And if I had not decided that I could run, I never would have become a marathoner. While we definitely have the greatest influence when it comes to our self-efficacy, everyone around us add to our belief (or lack thereof) in our ability to succeed. So, remember to surround yourself with those who believe in you and encourage you to go after your dreams. And if you ever doubt yourself, just remember that I believe in you. After all, if I could run a marathon, become a doctor, and write a book, anything is possible.

While we cannot control how other people act or feel, what we can do is remember that other people do influence our own self-efficacy. One of my favorite sayings is the African proverb, *it takes a village to raise a child.* I wrote this in my first book, *Composing Composition: The Art of the Written Word,* as well as in my doctoral dissertation, and I even mentioned it during my doctoral candidacy interviews (Ryan 2019). I love it because it tells us that none of us have gotten to where we are today solely because of ourselves. My parents choosing to support my love for writing, praising me, getting me tutors when I needed them, and teachers who were knowledgeable, were a huge part of why I am where I am today.

I urge you to remember, however, that just because we have supportive teachers, parents, and peers that does not automatically mean we do not have to put in any work. In fact, it is our relationship with ourselves that we need to work on the most. And even with parents who supported me with writing, I can never forget how long it took me to realize that I liked (and was good at) math as well. At the root of it, we need to focus on building our foundation on being successful. We should never forget that anyone who does not seem to support us could also bring down our self-efficacy. So, it is our job to only let those who support us and make us thrive influence our belief in our ability to succeed.

If we ignore this idea of self-efficacy, how you feel about writing? Is it something you enjoy or something you struggle with? Once you have an idea as to how you feel, I want you to consider why you feel this way.

Take me, for example. For years, decades really, I could not imagine the idea of ever understanding math. Perhaps the idea that women struggle with, and are the rarity, in Science Technology

Engineering, and Math (STEM) classes was a stereotype I had fallen victim to. This is completely false. The idea that an entire gender cannot succeed in a subject is laughable. My mother has a bachelor's degree in math, a master's in information technology (IT), and works in the technology field. And yet, whenever people asked me how I felt about math my answers were one of the following: *It is hard. It is confusing. I do not get it. I cannot do math.*

In fact, it was not until I was in my doctoral program that I realized how much I actually enjoyed numbers. I took a qualitative subject such as self-efficacy and chose to view it in a quantitative way by statistically analyzing my data for my dissertation. In my Quantitative Research Methods course, I remember being shocked that I got the first answer right. It felt like a fluke, as if I somehow had luck on my side and it was pure coincidence. Then, I got another question correct and I felt like I had tricked the system into winning. Surely this could not mean I understood the material was my first thought. It was surprising, but also very freeing and liberating when I finally realized that I had always understood numbers. And the person who had kept me from realizing this for a couple of decades was me.

We so often feel like the imposter conning the system; hence, the prevalence of imposter syndrome and its very real impact on our success. So often we feel like we cannot be good at something because we have decided we are not good at it, or worse, someone else has decided that for us (a former teacher, a parent, a friend, society, etc.).

So, getting back to our original question, how do you feel when it comes to writing? Is this the subject you are amazing at or is this the subject you struggle with? And if you are an amazing writer, why do you feel this way? Who told you that you were? Who made you feel like a rock star writer? And if you are on the other end of the spectrum, why do you feel this way? Who made you believe you were anything other than the world's greatest writer?

These may not be answers you have immediately, but I want you to take time to delve into why you feel this way. After all, Eleanor Roosevelt stated that, "No one can make you feel inferior without your consent," but I have always also believed that no one can make you feel like you are incapable of doing something without your consent.

The R-Model and The Motivation Theory

When I wrote my doctoral dissertation, I created something called the R-model, a self-efficacy framework. This theoretical framework looks at the student's past and present, and how Variables A (the student's belief) and Variables B (the student's demographics and interests) impacted their self-efficacy when it came to writing. As you consider your own self-efficacy, I urge you to take into consideration this model and how it impacts your individual circumstances.

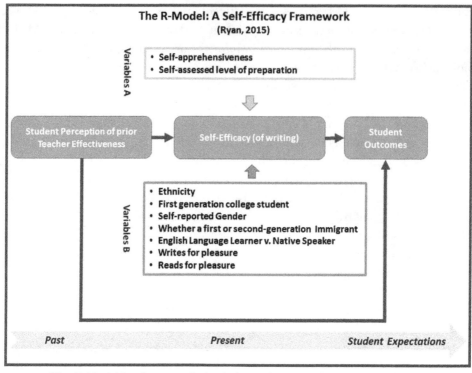

{The R-Model is a framework that helps us better understand self-efficacy.}

The Motivation Theory, on the other hand, theorized that low-risk assignments (short readings, journals, free writes, and assignments) paired with positive feedback from the instructor, along with material that gained the student's interest and engagement, and an understanding of the student's background, would help promote success. As an instructor, it is our job to know our students, understand their interests, and learn how we can help them. And as a student it is important to know how our interests, demographics, and beliefs can impact our success.

Missy's Memoir

{Who has impacted your self-efficacy?}

Missy and Kaley find that it is the first of the month again. While they are both working students, they wish they had a job that paid a little more. Missy works in retail, helping women buy new wardrobes, while Kaley works as a hostess at the neighborhood burger joint.

"You know," Missy begins as the two friends finish signing each of their rent checks. "In my business class we learned some of the benefits of working for yourself."

"That sounds lovely," Kaley admits. "I'm exhausted. Class started at 8:00 a.m. today, and went on until 4:00 p.m. I had lunch while walking from one class to the next. And my break between school and work is the hour I have to place my backpack down, change, write a check that is basically my entire paycheck, and then work until we close at 1:00 a.m. I like the idea of working from home and having flexible hours."

"Plus, who is a better boss than us?" Missy laughs. "I also learned that you could make a lot of money, depending on your business and how successful you are. Maybe this is what we need to do."

"I like the idea," Kaley begins. "But a) what would we do? And b) could we actually do this? It is not like we have a business degree or any other type of expertise."

"Well, I am halfway through this business class," Missy says. "But many small businesses fail within their first year. And you need to invest your own money or get investors to do that, and who would do that for two college students? Plus, my professor has a graduate degree and only recently began his business. We have not even finished college yet."

"I have heard of businesses started by students our age," Kaley adds. "And there are entrepreneurs who have dropped out of school and watched their business become super successful. But who would invest in us? We are not business majors who plan to get an MBA next or have a specialized expertise in something."

"That is true," Missy admits. "And as a business owner you need to wear many hats and I am not sure I even know how to wear just one of those hats. I think we should ask my teacher. He has office hours right now."

The two girls walk to Missy's professor's office where they see their friends, Rowdy and Brody.

"Hey, guys," Missy says. "How are you?"

"Good," Rowdy replies. "We are here to chat with Professor Green on how to launch a tech start-up. We have an idea but no clue how to make it a reality."

Kaley beams. "Oh, my goodness, so do we! We are not sure what type of business we want to run yet, but we know we want to become our own bosses."

The four begin asking Professor Green how they can become entrepreneurs, but are surprised by his response.

"I am glad the four of you are interested in a business, but first you need a clear vision of what you will be creating."

"A tech start-up," Brody pipes up.

"But what will this start-up do?" He asks. "Is it a social media site or a company that will build computers or phones?"

"We are not sure yet, Professor," Kaley replies.

"And you, my dear, how many business classes have you taken?" He asks Kaley.

"None," she replies sheepishly.

"You need to learn then. Whether you take a class here next semester or read about it online or in books. Our campus has a lot of resources to help, but I think all four of you need to take some time to focus on school and a business plan before you can do anything else at all. I mean, I waited until I was 35 and had a graduate degree in entrepreneurship before I began my first company. And even then, it failed. Many businesses fail. It is a lot of blood, sweat, and tears. It is a lot of work. Running a company means working 24/7 instead of just 9 to 5. Take time to decide if this is the right path for each of you."

The four friends thank Professor Green and head out.

"Well, I guess it is time for work. Have a good evening, guys." Kaley says. It is clear from their faces that the four no longer have the same excitement they had earlier that afternoon at the thought of creating their own company.

"Wait," Missy replies. "We just need five minutes together."

"Sure," Kaley responds. "I have five minutes." Rowdy and Brody nod in agreement. The four friends head to a table nearby and sit under a large oak tree.

"How is everyone?" Missy asks.

"Fine," Rowdy replies. "But disappointed I do not have a business mindset."

"Same," Brody adds. "I really thought that R and I could do this. I thought we could create something that the world needed before they knew they needed it. That is the entrepreneur's dream, after all."

"This was never even my dream," Kaley begins. "But I have never felt so inadequate. There are business owners who can create successful companies without going to school. Professor Green just made me feel like I was not good enough."

"How do you feel, Miss?" Rowdy asks.

"The same way," she answers. "Inadequate and not good enough. But I realized something when Professor Green was speaking."

"What was it?" Kaley inquires.

"All semester I have learned from the three of you. You have helped boost my confidence and self-efficacy, as well as understand my imposter syndrome and fear. So, why are we allowing one person to make us feel like we cannot be successful? Maybe Professor Green's first business failed because he did not have a high enough self-efficacy," she states.

"And maybe it failed because he is not us," Brody adds.

"I used to think that we were the only ones who could impact our self-efficacy. After all, the word itself has self in it. But other people can affect it as well. We took Professor Green's experience and advice to heart. And while I think he said everything to help us, it ended up impacting our confidence instead. I do agree that we should think about what kind of business we want first and learn more about how to start a business. But let us not give up on our dream just because Professor Green thinks we are not yet ready. I think he believes that because he was not ready at our age, that means no one else is either."

"You are so right," Kaley admits. "Thank you for this perspective, Miss."

"You are wise, Missy," Rowdy adds. "Now you are the one who is teaching us."

Brody nods in agreement. "Can we plan to meet up this weekend and begin brainstorming some business ideas together"

"Yes," Missy exclaims!

"I love it," Kaley adds. "But now I have to get to work. Have a great evening, everyone." She hugs everyone goodbye, and the four friends head out.

Workbook Questions

1. Why does Professor Green's advice lower Rowdy, Missy, Kaley, and Brody's self-efficacy when it comes to their entrepreneurial dreams? Is his advice accurate? If so, to whom (to him, to them, to other students, to other entrepreneurs, etc.)? Why or why not? Explain.
2. Why are Missy and Kaley so self-apprehensive to create a small business? Where in this story did their low self-efficacy come into play and sabotage this idea of leaving their retail and restaurant jobs? And how do we do things like this in our day-to-day lives?

{Small dogs. Big personalities}.

In the play, *A Midsummer Night's Dream*, William Shakespeare writes, "And though she be but little, she is fierce." I never thought much about that quote, yet once I adopted small dogs I realized how true it is. There is truly something incredible about small dogs and their big personalities. My nine-and-a-half- pound Chihuahua rescue shows me every day that true confidence, high self-efficacy, low self-apprehensiveness, and an inherent belief in oneself stems from within. Almost anyone who has had a small dog is likely familiar with this concept. Small dogs rarely fear big dogs and will bark at them to either play or out of their own self-protection; their human counterparts are typically the ones who fear that the 90-pound dog will accidentally hurt their pup who is ten times smaller. Small dogs believe in their hearts and minds that they are big and try to make themselves look larger than they are whether it is through their bark or through their attitude. They never question if someone will call them out for being smaller than they portray themselves. And thus, the one who never doubts himself, always believes in himself, and has the concept of authentic confidence down to a T is my dog.

After reading these last five chapters, you may feel like you should have high self-efficacy. But self-efficacy does not work this way. For example, if I exercised today, does that mean I never need to work out again? You are likely shaking your head no, as you recognize that a work-out one day will not be enough for a lifetime. In fact, a single workout will likely not even give someone the permanent results they may want such as muscle building, muscle toning, or weight loss. In that same way, we know that eating clean once a week will not undo the damage caused by making poor food choices for the other six days of the week or studying the night before an exam will likely not help us retain the knowledge from a class the same way we would if we studied gradually for the test.

These examples are to remind us that self-efficacy is similar; it is something we need to work on every single day. There likely will be days when you wake up and cannot imagine writing a strong paper or just writing in general. There will be days when I cannot imagine being able to calculate another number. And, of course, we will all have days when we may not want to work out or eat a healthy diet. I want to remind you that this is normal. There are likely days when the last thing we want to do is exercise, but the popular suggestion has always been to start exercising for 10 minutes. If you still feel too tired, bored, or uninterested in it, you can stop. But almost always, once you have laced up your sneakers and begun to work up a sweat, you will be ready to complete your workout. In that same way, if you ever feel too tired at the thought of writing a paper, start small. Tell yourself you will simply create an outline or a mind map. Give yourself 10 minutes in front of the computer without any distractions (such as your phone, your pet, the Internet, etc.). If you still do not want to write, then maybe this is not the right time for you. Take a break and come back to it later. And the same is true of your mindset.

I want you to remember this for the rest of your life. While you have finished reading this book, the true understanding of your mindset is still left for you to understand. By digging deeper into your psyche and taking time to journal all 101 prompts (in their current order, out of order, one day at a time, or over several months or years), these prompts will help you better grasp why you feel the way you feel and how you can reframe your mindset to become a strong, more successful writer (or wherever else you want to transform your self-efficacy). It is also easy to forget the importance of believing in yourself and your incredible capabilities. But you should not. It is important to remember to keep your self-efficacy high; after all, if you do not believe in yourself, who will? I recommend you take time to journal through all the prompts in this book and really consider what it means for you and your own belief in yourself. And if you decide to look at it from a lens outside of writing, feel free to substitute the words for your other interests such as creating a company, traveling the world, creating a multimillion-dollar net worth, or whatever else your dreams might be. My only wish for you is to never forget those dreams and wishes, and someday make them into a reality. My mantra for years has been: *Stop dreaming and start doing.* And with that, I wish for each of us to have that big personality a small dog has, to never forget our dreams, and most importantly, to start doing.

All my best,
Dr. R

PART 2

101 Journal Prompts

1. How do you feel about your ability to write and about writing in general? Why?

_____

_____

_____

_____

_____

_____

_____

_____

_____

_____

_____

_____

_____

_____

_____

_____

_____

_____

_____

_____

_____

_____

_____

_____

_____

_____

_____

_____

_____

_____

2. How do you feel about your authentic confidence? Explain.

_____

_____

_____

_____

_____

_____

_____

_____

_____

_____

_____

_____

_____

_____

_____

_____

_____

_____

_____

_____

_____

_____

_____

_____

_____

_____

_____

_____

_____

_____

_____

3. How do you define imposter syndrome and how does it impact your life? Why do you feel it affects you this way? Explain.

_____

_____

_____

_____

_____

_____

_____

_____

_____

_____

_____

_____

_____

_____

_____

_____

_____

_____

_____

_____

_____

_____

_____

_____

_____

4. Why do you believe you struggle with writing or why do you find writing to be a subject that comes naturally to you? Explain.

_____

_____

_____

_____

_____

_____

_____

_____

_____

_____

_____

_____

_____

_____

_____

_____

_____

_____

_____

_____

_____

_____

_____

_____

_____

_____

_____

5. Who do you believe can make you a stronger writer? Why?

_____

_____

_____

_____

_____

_____

_____

_____

_____

_____

_____

_____

_____

_____

_____

_____

_____

_____

_____

_____

_____

_____

_____

_____

_____

_____

_____

6. How do you feel self-efficacy influences your success with writing? How do you feel it impacts your success in other areas of your life? Explain.

_____

_____

_____

_____

_____

_____

_____

_____

_____

_____

_____

_____

_____

_____

_____

_____

_____

_____

_____

_____

_____

_____

_____

_____

_____

_____

_____

_____

_____

7. Why do you want to work on your self-efficacy? Why did you buy this book and how do you utilize it? Explain.

_____

_____

_____

_____

_____

_____

_____

_____

_____

_____

_____

_____

_____

_____

_____

_____

_____

_____

_____

_____

_____

_____

_____

_____

_____

_____

8. What areas of writing do you feel you struggle with (grammar, thesis statements, utilizing outside sources, etc.)? Why?

_____

_____

_____

_____

_____

_____

_____

_____

_____

_____

_____

_____

_____

_____

_____

_____

_____

_____

_____

_____

_____

_____

_____

_____

_____

_____

9. What areas of self-efficacy and self-confidence do you feel you struggle with? Why? Explain.

_____

_____

_____

_____

_____

_____

_____

_____

_____

_____

_____

_____

_____

_____

_____

_____

_____

_____

_____

_____

_____

_____

_____

_____

_____

_____

_____

_____

_____

10. Do you walk into most classes with the belief that you will succeed or fail at the end of the course? Why do you believe you feel this way?

_____

_____

_____

_____

_____

_____

_____

_____

_____

_____

_____

_____

_____

_____

_____

_____

_____

_____

_____

_____

_____

_____

_____

_____

_____

_____

_____

_____

_____

_____

11. What is your perception on how your current or previous English teacher felt about your ability to write a strong academic paper? Why do you feel this way? Do you think it speaks more to how you feel about your ability to write or how your teacher felt? Explain.

_____

_____

_____

_____

_____

_____

_____

_____

_____

_____

_____

_____

_____

_____

_____

_____

_____

_____

_____

_____

_____

_____

_____

_____

_____

12. Do you feel your prior or current teacher's perception of your ability to write well has impacted (either in a positive or negative way) your ability to write? Why? How?

_____

_____

_____

_____

_____

_____

_____

_____

_____

_____

_____

_____

_____

_____

_____

_____

_____

_____

_____

_____

_____

_____

_____

_____

_____

_____

13. Do you believe that with enough time and hard work, you can write a strong paper? Do you believe that this combination of time and effort can lead you to success with anything? Why or why not?

_____

_____

_____

_____

_____

_____

_____

_____

_____

_____

_____

_____

_____

_____

_____

_____

_____

_____

_____

_____

_____

_____

_____

_____

14. Do you feel that practice makes perfect and that with enough practice writing, anyone can be a stronger wordsmith? Explain.

_____

_____

_____

_____

_____

_____

_____

_____

_____

_____

_____

_____

_____

_____

_____

_____

_____

_____

_____

_____

_____

_____

_____

_____

_____

15. Do you feel confident in your ability to succeed in your degree of choice and in your career path? How about in the general education classes required to earn said degree such as English? How come? Explain.

_____

_____

_____

_____

_____

_____

_____

_____

_____

_____

_____

_____

_____

_____

_____

_____

_____

_____

_____

_____

_____

_____

_____

_____

_____

16. Do you believe talent is something we are born with or something we create? Why?

_____

_____

_____

_____

_____

_____

_____

_____

_____

_____

_____

_____

_____

_____

_____

_____

_____

_____

_____

_____

_____

_____

_____

_____

_____

_____

_____

_____

17. Do you stick to your goals, even if they turn out to be more challenging than you had originally expected them to be? Explain.

_____

_____

_____

_____

_____

_____

_____

_____

_____

_____

_____

_____

_____

_____

_____

_____

_____

_____

_____

_____

_____

_____

_____

_____

_____

18. What do you believe you are really great at? What do you feel you struggle with? Why? And have you put more time and effort and/or have more passion for the thing you feel you are successful at than the thing you struggle with? How come? Could this influence your success? Explain.

_____

_____

_____

_____

_____

_____

_____

_____

_____

_____

_____

_____

_____

_____

_____

_____

_____

_____

_____

_____

_____

_____

_____

19. What motivates you? Why? Explain.

_____

_____

_____

_____

_____

_____

_____

_____

_____

_____

_____

_____

_____

_____

_____

_____

_____

_____

_____

_____

_____

_____

_____

_____

_____

_____

_____

_____

_____

_____

20. We have all likely heard of the various types of intelligence such as being street smart versus book smart. Taking this idea into account, do you believe you are book smart? Why or why not? What type of intelligence do you identify with most? Explain.

_____

_____

_____

_____

_____

_____

_____

_____

_____

_____

_____

_____

_____

_____

_____

_____

_____

_____

_____

_____

_____

_____

_____

_____

_____

_____

21. Do you enjoy writing? Before you answer that, think about the various forms of writing that exists (creative writing, text messages, emails, letters, etc.). Do you enjoy any of these forms of writing? If so, why? If not, why not?

_____

_____

_____

_____

_____

_____

_____

_____

_____

_____

_____

_____

_____

_____

_____

_____

_____

_____

_____

_____

_____

_____

_____

_____

_____

22. In your opinion, what makes for a successful student and/or writer? Do you identify with either or both of these titles? Why? Explain.

_____

_____

_____

_____

_____

_____

_____

_____

_____

_____

_____

_____

_____

_____

_____

_____

_____

_____

_____

_____

_____

_____

_____

_____

_____

_____

_____

_____

_____

23. What makes you feel confident about submitting an academic paper? Is it writing about a topic you know well, working on a paper for a long time, or something else entirely? Explain.

_____

_____

_____

_____

_____

_____

_____

_____

_____

_____

_____

_____

_____

_____

_____

_____

_____

_____

_____

_____

_____

_____

_____

_____

_____

_____

_____

_____

24. What is the purpose of writing academic papers (aside from earning a degree)? Explain.

_____

_____

_____

_____

_____

_____

_____

_____

_____

_____

_____

_____

_____

_____

_____

_____

_____

_____

_____

_____

_____

_____

_____

_____

_____

_____

_____

_____

_____

25. They say comparison is the thief of joy. Do you ever compare yourself to others, especially when it comes to your writing? How can you avoid doing that in the future if you do this, and if you don't, how do you avoid it? Explain.

_____

_____

_____

_____

_____

_____

_____

_____

_____

_____

_____

_____

_____

_____

_____

_____

_____

_____

_____

_____

_____

_____

_____

_____

_____

_____

_____

26. Why are you interested in strengthening your skills when it comes to the art of the written word (e.g. to earn a degree, for your career, personal improvement, etc.)? Explain.

_____

_____

_____

_____

_____

_____

_____

_____

_____

_____

_____

_____

_____

_____

_____

_____

_____

_____

_____

_____

_____

_____

_____

_____

_____

_____

_____

_____

_____

_____

27. One of my favorite sayings is the African proverb, *it takes a village to raise a child*. Based on this idea, who is part of your village? Why are they on your team? How do they help you with your goals and dreams? And how can they help you improve your confidence and self-efficacy, as well as your writing? Explain.

_____

_____

_____

_____

_____

_____

_____

_____

_____

_____

_____

_____

_____

_____

_____

_____

_____

_____

_____

_____

_____

_____

_____

28. What do you do on a daily basis to work towards your goals (e.g. follow a running schedule to train for a marathon, eat clean to lose weight, practice the guitar to become a better
guitarist, and so on)? Have these habits helped you succeed (e.g. practicing the guitar has
made you into a stronger player)? If so, have you created a habit when it comes to your
writing skills? Why or why not?

29. Imagine you play an instrument and meet with your teacher once a week where you learn a song you will perform for him or her the next week. How do you feel when you have to play the song if you did not practice all week? How about if you practice once a day, every day? And what if you spend 30 minutes a day daily? Do you feel more confident with more practice? Do you believe you play the song better with the practice? And do you think it would be the same with writing? Why? Explain.

_____

_____

_____

_____

_____

_____

_____

_____

_____

_____

_____

_____

_____

_____

_____

_____

_____

_____

_____

_____

_____

30. When do you believe you will be a strong writer (e.g. when you pass an English class you are taking, earn a degree, write a book, etc.)? Do you already feel this way or do you believe you still need to work on your writing skills? If so, why are you already a strong writer? And if not, what do you need to do to become a strong wordsmith in your eyes? Explain.

31. In five words, how would you describe your skills as a writer? How many of these words were positive and how many were negative? Why do you believe you used these terms, and why are they so positive or negative? Either way, do you think they are accurate when it comes to your actual work or accurate when it comes to your mindset about your capability to write well? Explain.

32. Do you identify as being a perfectionist? If so, how does this impact your ability as an author? If not, how do you avoid perfectionism while still holding your writing to high, but attainable, standards? Explain.

33. What aspect of writing do you feel is your strongest skill (e.g. creating creative titles, strong thesis statements, a great structure, etc.)? Why? Explain.

34. What aspect of writing do you find the toughest (e.g. writing an attention grabbing hook, utilizing proper grammar, following MLA format, etc.)? Why do you believe it is such a challenge for you? Explain.

_____

_____

_____

_____

_____

_____

_____

_____

_____

_____

_____

_____

_____

_____

_____

_____

_____

_____

_____

_____

_____

_____

_____

_____

_____

_____

35. What scares you the most about writing? Why? And how do you feel this fear has impacted your writing abilities? Explain.

_____

_____

_____

_____

_____

_____

_____

_____

_____

_____

_____

_____

_____

_____

_____

_____

_____

_____

_____

_____

_____

_____

_____

_____

_____

_____

_____

_____

_____

_____

36. How has your writing transformed over the course of your life? How do you think it will continue to transform in the next year, five years, ten years, and your lifetime? Explain.

_____

_____

_____

_____

_____

_____

_____

_____

_____

_____

_____

_____

_____

_____

_____

_____

_____

_____

_____

_____

_____

_____

_____

_____

_____

_____

37. What is your proudest accomplishment? Did you ever worry you would fail while working towards this goal? Explain.

_____

_____

_____

_____

_____

_____

_____

_____

_____

_____

_____

_____

_____

_____

_____

_____

_____

_____

_____

_____

_____

_____

_____

_____

_____

38. How does writing (all forms of it: scholarly texts, poetry, fiction, emails, letters, etc.) challenge you? Explain.

39. In your opinion, what is the purpose of writing (look at it from a general lens and then focus on the various types of writing from composition to creative writing)? Why?

_____

_____

_____

_____

_____

_____

_____

_____

_____

_____

_____

_____

_____

_____

_____

_____

_____

_____

_____

_____

_____

_____

_____

_____

_____

40. What is your definition of being a successful writer? Why does this make one successful in your opinion? Explain.

_____

_____

_____

_____

_____

_____

_____

_____

_____

_____

_____

_____

_____

_____

_____

_____

_____

_____

_____

_____

_____

_____

_____

_____

_____

_____

_____

_____

_____

_____

41. What is your definition of failure when it comes to writing? Why does this make one fail in your opinion? Explain.

_____

_____

_____

_____

_____

_____

_____

_____

_____

_____

_____

_____

_____

_____

_____

_____

_____

_____

_____

_____

_____

_____

_____

_____

_____

_____

_____

_____

42. Have you ever skipped (or considered skipping) submitting a writing assignment for class or work because of the fear of failure? Did it end up helping or hurting you? Why did you do this or consider doing this? Explain.

---

43. Does writing stress you out? How so? Why? Explain.

_____

_____

_____

_____

_____

_____

_____

_____

_____

_____

_____

_____

_____

_____

_____

_____

_____

_____

_____

_____

_____

_____

_____

_____

_____

_____

_____

_____

_____

44. How much do you believe stress plays a role in your writing? Do you feel it affects your writing when you are stressed over a certain assignment? Explain.

_____

_____

_____

_____

_____

_____

_____

_____

_____

_____

_____

_____

_____

_____

_____

_____

_____

_____

_____

_____

_____

_____

_____

_____

_____

_____

_____

_____

_____

45. Why are you reading this book? Why are you interested in improving your self-efficacy and your writing? Explain.

_____

_____

_____

_____

_____

_____

_____

_____

_____

_____

_____

_____

_____

_____

_____

_____

_____

_____

_____

_____

_____

_____

_____

_____

_____

46. Do you ever procrastinate? If so, why do you believe you do so? Does it stem from fear, stress, a lack of confidence, or something else? Explain.

_____

_____

_____

_____

_____

_____

_____

_____

_____

_____

_____

_____

_____

_____

_____

_____

_____

_____

_____

_____

_____

_____

_____

_____

_____

_____

_____

_____

_____

_____

47. When are you the most productive? When are you least productive? It can be a time of day, a time of year, or a type of assignment you are working on. Explain.

48. Who are you? How would you describe yourself? How long did it take you to call yourself a writer or do you not consider yourself one? Why? And how often do you write? Daily, weekly, monthly? Remember text messages, emails, lists, letters, poetry, song lyrics, etc. are all a form of writing. Explain.

_____

_____

_____

_____

_____

_____

_____

_____

_____

_____

_____

_____

_____

_____

_____

_____

_____

_____

_____

_____

_____

_____

_____

_____

_____

49. Do you believe you are a better writer today than you were yesterday? How about a year ago? Why or why not? Explain.

_____

_____

_____

_____

_____

_____

_____

_____

_____

_____

_____

_____

_____

_____

_____

_____

_____

_____

_____

_____

_____

_____

_____

_____

_____

_____

_____

_____

_____

_____

50. What do you have the power to choose? How long did it take for you to state your self-efficacy? Why do you think it took so long to think of it? Explain.

_____

_____

_____

_____

_____

_____

_____

_____

_____

_____

_____

_____

_____

_____

_____

_____

_____

_____

_____

_____

_____

_____

_____

_____

_____

_____

_____

51. Has failure ever been a good thing in your life? Has failure, when it comes to writing, ever been a blessing in disguise? How so? Explain.

_____

_____

_____

_____

_____

_____

_____

_____

_____

_____

_____

_____

_____

_____

_____

_____

_____

_____

_____

_____

_____

_____

_____

_____

_____

The Thinking Problem

52. How do you feel and react to constructive criticism when it comes to your writing, as well as in general? Explain.

_____

_____

_____

_____

_____

_____

_____

_____

_____

_____

_____

_____

_____

_____

_____

_____

_____

_____

_____

_____

_____

_____

_____

_____

_____

_____

_____

_____

53. How do you react to a compliment when it comes to your writing, as well as in general? Do you accept it or deny it? Explain.

_____

_____

_____

_____

_____

_____

_____

_____

_____

_____

_____

_____

_____

_____

_____

_____

_____

_____

_____

_____

_____

_____

_____

_____

_____

_____

54. Do you believe that growth comes from pushing yourself to your limit and becoming slightly uncomfortable? Why? If so, how does this impact your writing? If not, why is it unnecessary to experience any discomfort in order to grow? Explain.

_____

_____

_____

_____

_____

_____

_____

_____

_____

_____

_____

_____

_____

_____

_____

_____

_____

_____

_____

_____

_____

_____

_____

_____

_____

_____

_____

55. Why did you choose your career and/or your degree? Do you think your confidence or self-efficacy impacted this/these decision(s)? Explain.

_____

_____

_____

_____

_____

_____

_____

_____

_____

_____

_____

_____

_____

_____

_____

_____

_____

_____

_____

_____

_____

_____

_____

_____

_____

_____

_____

_____

_____

56. What was the best lesson you ever learned on how to become a stronger writer? Why do you feel this was the best? How did it help you? Did it change your mindset, your actual writing ability, both, or something else? Explain.

_____

_____

_____

_____

_____

_____

_____

_____

_____

_____

_____

_____

_____

_____

_____

_____

_____

_____

_____

_____

_____

_____

_____

57. What are you most proud of that does not have to do with any sort of accomplishment or achievement? For example, you may be proud of your kind heart, great friendships, or your love of learning. Do you think your mindset impacted this in anyway? If so, how did your self-efficacy play a role in this? If not, why not?

58. What do you read? How much do you read? And do you believe that strong writers are avid readers? Why?

_____

_____

_____

_____

_____

_____

_____

_____

_____

_____

_____

_____

_____

_____

_____

_____

_____

_____

_____

_____

_____

_____

_____

_____

_____

_____

The Thinking Problem

59. What makes you feel confident? Why? Explain.

_____

_____

_____

_____

_____

_____

_____

_____

_____

_____

_____

_____

_____

_____

_____

_____

_____

_____

_____

_____

_____

_____

_____

_____

_____

_____

_____

_____

_____

_____

60. What takes away your confidence? Why? Explain.

_____

_____

_____

_____

_____

_____

_____

_____

_____

_____

_____

_____

_____

_____

_____

_____

_____

_____

_____

_____

_____

_____

_____

_____

_____

_____

_____

_____

_____

_____

_____

61. What habits build up your confidence? Why? Explain.

_____
_____
_____
_____
_____
_____
_____
_____
_____
_____
_____
_____
_____
_____
_____
_____
_____
_____
_____
_____
_____
_____
_____
_____
_____
_____
_____
_____
_____
_____
_____

62. Once you finish writing a paper, do you feel it is good enough to submit? What makes it good enough? Why?

_____

_____

_____

_____

_____

_____

_____

_____

_____

_____

_____

_____

_____

_____

_____

_____

_____

_____

_____

_____

_____

_____

_____

_____

_____

_____

_____

_____

_____

63. What do you believe you are capable of achieving? How long did it take you to state being a strong writer? Why do you think this was the case? Explain.

_____

_____

_____

_____

_____

_____

_____

_____

_____

_____

_____

_____

_____

_____

_____

_____

_____

_____

_____

_____

_____

_____

_____

_____

_____

_____

_____

64. Do you believe that perfectionism or fear is holding you back from success? Why? How can you overcome this? Explain.

65. Do you believe in progress over perfection (that it is better to try even if your end result is imperfect) or that avoiding failure is the best method for succeeding? Why? Explain.

_____

_____

_____

_____

_____

_____

_____

_____

_____

_____

_____

_____

_____

_____

_____

_____

_____

_____

_____

_____

_____

_____

_____

_____

_____

_____

_____

_____

66. When you finish a writing assignment, how long does it take you to think about what you did well? How long does it take you to consider what you could strengthen? Why do you believe this is the case? Explain.

_____

_____

_____

_____

_____

_____

_____

_____

_____

_____

_____

_____

_____

_____

_____

_____

_____

_____

_____

_____

_____

_____

_____

_____

_____

_____

_____

67. Whether you write an A paper or an essay that earns a failing grade, what challenged you about the assignment and what did you learn from it? Do you think they are both important learning experiences? Why? Explain.

_____

_____

_____

_____

_____

_____

_____

_____

_____

_____

_____

_____

_____

_____

_____

_____

_____

_____

_____

_____

_____

_____

_____

_____

_____

_____

_____

_____

_____

68. Whether you love your English class and want to major in the subject or you are simply in it for the general education course or to strengthen your writing skills, what do you like about writing? And what do you specifically like about academic writing? Explain.

_____

_____

_____

_____

_____

_____

_____

_____

_____

_____

_____

_____

_____

_____

_____

_____

_____

_____

_____

_____

_____

_____

_____

_____

_____

_____

_____

_____

The Thinking Problem

198

69. If you could become an expert at anything today, what would you choose? And why would you choose this subject? And how would becoming an expert at writing help you in your daily life? Explain.

_____

_____

_____

_____

_____

_____

_____

_____

_____

_____

_____

_____

_____

_____

_____

_____

_____

_____

_____

_____

_____

_____

_____

_____

_____

_____

_____

_____

_____

70. If you knew there was no way to fail, what would you do? Now that you have determined it, are you doing it? Explain. And if you are not, why not?

_____

_____

_____

_____

_____

_____

_____

_____

_____

_____

_____

_____

_____

_____

_____

_____

_____

_____

_____

_____

_____

_____

_____

_____

_____

_____

_____

_____

_____

71. What did you learn from your last writing assignment? It can be something you did well or something you learned you needed to work on. Do you think it was important to learn this? Why? Explain.

_____

_____

_____

_____

_____

_____

_____

_____

_____

_____

_____

_____

_____

_____

_____

_____

_____

_____

_____

_____

_____

_____

_____

_____

_____

_____

72. Do you believe you can write a strong essay when you only have a limited amount of time (such as an in-class essay)? Why or why not? Explain.

_____

_____

_____

_____

_____

_____

_____

_____

_____

_____

_____

_____

_____

_____

_____

_____

_____

_____

_____

_____

_____

_____

_____

_____

_____

_____

_____

_____

_____

_____

_____

_____

_____

_____

_____

73. Many people find that starting an assignment, especially a paper, is the toughest part of writing. Do you find it hard to begin writing? If so, is it due to the desire to procrastinate or because of an actual struggle with writing your assignment (such as not understanding the prompt)? Why? Explain.

_____

_____

_____

_____

_____

_____

_____

_____

_____

_____

_____

_____

_____

_____

_____

_____

_____

_____

_____

_____

_____

_____

_____

_____

74. Do you find it easy to be creative and come up with an interesting and engaging hook to capture your reader's attention? What about a strong thesis statement, aka your Global Positioning System (GPS) or roadmap for your essay? Why do you feel this way? Could your self-efficacy have impacted these beliefs? Explain.

_____

_____

_____

_____

_____

_____

_____

_____

_____

_____

_____

_____

_____

_____

_____

_____

_____

_____

_____

_____

_____

_____

75. Do you find writing prompts and readings interesting and engaging in your English classes (prior or current)? Do you feel that if they are interesting, you tend to be more interested in writing? And do you think your mindset could help you write a stronger paper, even if you do not love the prompt? Why? Explain.

76. Do you attend a class believing there is no reason you will get any grade lower than an A? If not an A, do you believe you will pass the class or earn the grade you want? Or do you start the semester worried about whether or not you will succeed? Why? Explain.

77. Do you share your paper with people while it is still a draft (a tutor, a friend, a family member, your professor, etc.)? Why or why not? Does fear of not having a strong paper deter you from sharing it with others and learning how to improve your work? Explain.

_____

_____

_____

_____

_____

_____

_____

_____

_____

_____

_____

_____

_____

_____

_____

_____

_____

_____

_____

_____

_____

_____

_____

_____

78. If you share your paper with others before submitting it, do you believe you will get helpful, constructive feedback? And if you do not share your paper, do you believe you could find someone who gives you important advice? Why do you feel this way? Do you think your mindset about both yourself and others impacts this belief? Explain.

_____

_____

_____

_____

_____

_____

_____

_____

_____

_____

_____

_____

_____

_____

_____

_____

_____

_____

_____

_____

_____

_____

_____

79. Do you believe that you can find any and all errors in a paper you write? Why or why not? Do you think your self-efficacy has any impact on this thought? Why? Explain.

_____

_____

_____

_____

_____

_____

_____

_____

_____

_____

_____

_____

_____

_____

_____

_____

_____

_____

_____

_____

_____

_____

_____

_____

_____

_____

_____

_____

80. Did you take a lot of grammar classes or writing courses in school? If so, do you feel it has helped strengthen your grammar and writing skills? If not, do you feel the lack of preparation has made you feel unsure about your grammatical and writing abilities? Based on this, do you think that furthering your knowledge on a topic can improve your self-efficacy? Explain.

_____

_____

_____

_____

_____

_____

_____

_____

_____

_____

_____

_____

_____

_____

_____

_____

_____

_____

_____

_____

_____

_____

81. Do you believe you can revise every draft of an essay and make it stronger each time? Why or why not? And do you think your mindset is part of the reason why your paper gets stronger with every new draft? Explain.

_____

_____

_____

_____

_____

_____

_____

_____

_____

_____

_____

_____

_____

_____

_____

_____

_____

_____

_____

_____

_____

_____

_____

_____

_____

_____

_____

_____

_____

_____

82. Do you find ways to motivate yourself to do an assignment that seems challenging or un-interesting to you? How so? If not, how do you complete the assignment or do you skip it entirely? And do you believe fear plays a role in this scenario? Explain.

_____

_____

_____

_____

_____

_____

_____

_____

_____

_____

_____

_____

_____

_____

_____

_____

_____

_____

_____

_____

_____

_____

_____

_____

_____

_____

83. When you get a case of writer's block, do you believe you can find a way to work around the issue? Why? And do you think that someone with a higher level of self-efficacy than you would feel differently? Explain.

_____

_____

_____

_____

_____

_____

_____

_____

_____

_____

_____

_____

_____

_____

_____

_____

_____

_____

_____

_____

_____

_____

_____

_____

_____

The Thinking Problem

84. Do you believe you can write a strong paper no matter what type of essay it is (e.g. persuade the reader in a persuasive essay, avoid bringing in opinion in a research paper, and analyze text for an analytical essay)? How come? How did you build this confidence? And if not, why do you not believe you are capable of doing so? Explain.

_____

_____

_____

_____

_____

_____

_____

_____

_____

_____

_____

_____

_____

_____

_____

_____

_____

_____

_____

_____

_____

_____

_____

_____

_____

85. Do you feel you can write vividly, painting a picture for your readers to see even if it is an abstract idea or a tough topic to explain? Why? How did you increase your self-efficacy to feel this way? Was it through small successes in the past, practicing the art of writing, or something else? Explain. And if not, why not?

_____

_____

_____

_____

_____

_____

_____

_____

_____

_____

_____

_____

_____

_____

_____

_____

_____

_____

_____

_____

_____

_____

_____

_____

_____

_____

_____

86. Do you feel that you write clear and easy-to-understand sentences or do you feel you deal with syntactical struggles such as run-on and fragmented sentences? Why? And how does this impact your belief in your ability as a writer? Explain.

_____

_____

_____

_____

_____

_____

_____

_____

_____

_____

_____

_____

_____

_____

_____

_____

_____

_____

_____

_____

_____

_____

_____

_____

_____

_____

_____

_____

_____

87. Do you worry about your writing when you have a tough teacher, reviewer, or evaluator looking over it? And what is your definition of tough? Explain.

_____

_____

_____

_____

_____

_____

_____

_____

_____

_____

_____

_____

_____

_____

_____

_____

_____

_____

_____

_____

_____

_____

_____

_____

_____

_____

_____

88. What is the best compliment you have ever been given about your writing skills? Why? And how long did it take you to remember this? Why do you feel you remembered it immediately or that it took you so long to remember? Explain.

_____

_____

_____

_____

_____

_____

_____

_____

_____

_____

_____

_____

_____

_____

_____

_____

_____

_____

_____

_____

_____

_____

_____

_____

_____

_____

_____

_____

89. Write down three things that makes your writing unique to you and only you. Why did you choose these three traits? Do you feel that they truly make your work unique compared to everyone else's writing? And how do you feel about your ability to be a strong writer when you remind yourself of these traits? Explain.

_____

_____

_____

_____

_____

_____

_____

_____

_____

_____

_____

_____

_____

_____

_____

_____

_____

_____

_____

_____

_____

_____

_____

_____

_____

_____

_____

_____

90. Do you feel your parents or guardians encouraged you to write as a child? Do you feel they still encourage you to write? And do you believe their encouragement has pushed you to become a stronger writer or that their lack of encouragement has stifled your interest and ability to write? Why? How? Explain.

_____

_____

_____

_____

_____

_____

_____

_____

_____

_____

_____

_____

_____

_____

_____

_____

_____

_____

_____

_____

_____

_____

_____

_____

_____

91. Do you believe that all your prior English teachers have motivated you to write and reminded you of your talent as a writer? If so, do you feel it has helped you become a stronger wordsmith? If not, do you feel that is part of why you feel writing is not your strong suit? Explain.

_____

_____

_____

_____

_____

_____

_____

_____

_____

_____

_____

_____

_____

_____

_____

_____

_____

_____

_____

_____

_____

_____

_____

_____

_____

92. If you are asked to tell a story about what you did last weekend, do you believe you could easily explain it to a few friends? Now imagine you had to write the story instead. Which would be harder for you? Why? How come? Explain.

_____

_____

_____

_____

_____

_____

_____

_____

_____

_____

_____

_____

_____

_____

_____

_____

_____

_____

_____

_____

_____

_____

_____

_____

_____

93. What sort of emotions do you feel when you write a paper? How about when you submit it? And lastly, how do you feel when you wait to get it back with a grade on it? Why do you think you feel this way? Explain.

_____

_____

_____

_____

_____

_____

_____

_____

_____

_____

_____

_____

_____

_____

_____

_____

_____

_____

_____

_____

_____

_____

_____

_____

_____

_____

_____

_____

_____

_____

_____

94. What is your definition of being a confident writer? Why? Do you feel you fit your description? Why or why not?

_____

_____

_____

_____

_____

_____

_____

_____

_____

_____

_____

_____

_____

_____

_____

_____

_____

_____

_____

_____

_____

_____

_____

_____

_____

_____

_____

95. How would you describe your writing (what you need to work on and what you like about it)? Is this how you would describe your best friend's writing? A stranger's writing? A classmate's writing? Why or why not?

_____

_____

_____

_____

_____

_____

_____

_____

_____

_____

_____

_____

_____

_____

_____

_____

_____

_____

_____

_____

_____

_____

_____

_____

_____

_____

_____

_____

96. What is your definition of success? What is your definition of failure? How come? Explain.

_____

_____

_____

_____

_____

_____

_____

_____

_____

_____

_____

_____

_____

_____

_____

_____

_____

_____

_____

_____

_____

_____

_____

_____

_____

_____

_____

_____

97. Describe your skills as a writer through someone else's eyes (your parent, partner, friend, teacher, etc.). Is this how you would describe your work as well? Why? Explain.

_____

_____

_____

_____

_____

_____

_____

_____

_____

_____

_____

_____

_____

_____

_____

_____

_____

_____

_____

_____

_____

_____

_____

_____

_____

_____

_____

98. What was the best paper you ever wrote? Why did you choose this one? Was it because of your grade or how much you enjoyed writing it? Explain.

_____

_____

_____

_____

_____

_____

_____

_____

_____

_____

_____

_____

_____

_____

_____

_____

_____

_____

_____

_____

_____

_____

_____

_____

_____

99. Think about the last paper you wrote or the last writing assignment you completed. How would you critique your work? What did you do well and what do you need to work on? How will you utilize this feedback in your current and future writing assignments? And why is it important to think about this with your work? Explain.

_____
_____
_____
_____
_____
_____
_____
_____
_____
_____
_____
_____
_____
_____
_____
_____
_____
_____
_____
_____

100. How does imposter syndrome impact your writing ability? What do you think would help you overcome this feeling? And if it does not impact your writing, why do you feel this could be the case? Explain.

_____

_____

_____

_____

_____

_____

_____

_____

_____

_____

_____

_____

_____

_____

_____

_____

_____

_____

_____

_____

_____

_____

_____

_____

101. Why does self-efficacy and writing matter to you? What steps do you want to take towards improving both your self-efficacy and your writing skills? Explain.

_____

_____

_____

_____

_____

_____

_____

_____

_____

_____

_____

_____

_____

_____

_____

_____

_____

_____

_____

_____

_____

_____

_____

_____

_____

_____

_____

_____

_____

REFERENCES

Alton, Larry. 2017. "Why Low Self-Esteem May Be Hurting You at Work." NBC News. November 15, 2017. https://www.nbcnews.com/better/business/why-low-self-esteem-may-be-hurting-your-career-ncna814156.

Bandura, Albert. 1997. Self Efficacy: The Exercise of Control. New York, NY: W.H. Freeman.

"Four in Ten Canadians (40%) Lack Confidence in Social Situations; Causing Many to Avoid Meeting New People." 2019. Ipsos.Com. January 24, 2019. https://www.ipsos.com/en-ca/news-polls/Four-in-Ten-Canadians-Lack-Confidence-in-Social-Situations.

Ryan, Paris. 2019. Composing Composition: The Art of the Written Word. Dubuque, IA: Great River Learning.

Spector, Nicole. 2018. "Smiling Can Trick Your Brain into Happiness – and Boost Your Health." Nbcnews.Com. January 10, 2018. https://www.nbcnews.com/better/health/smiling-can-trick-your-brain-happiness-boost-your-health-ncna822591.

Sandlier, Allison. 2020. "Most Americans Admit They're Not Comfortable in Their Own Skin." New York Post, February 18, 2020. https://nypost.com/2020/02/18/most-americans-admit-theyre-not-comfortable-in-their-own-skin/.

CPSIA information can be obtained
at www.ICGtesting.com
Printed in the USA
FSHW021819110122
87549FS